GHOST

Building an Architectural Vision
Brian MacKay-Lyons

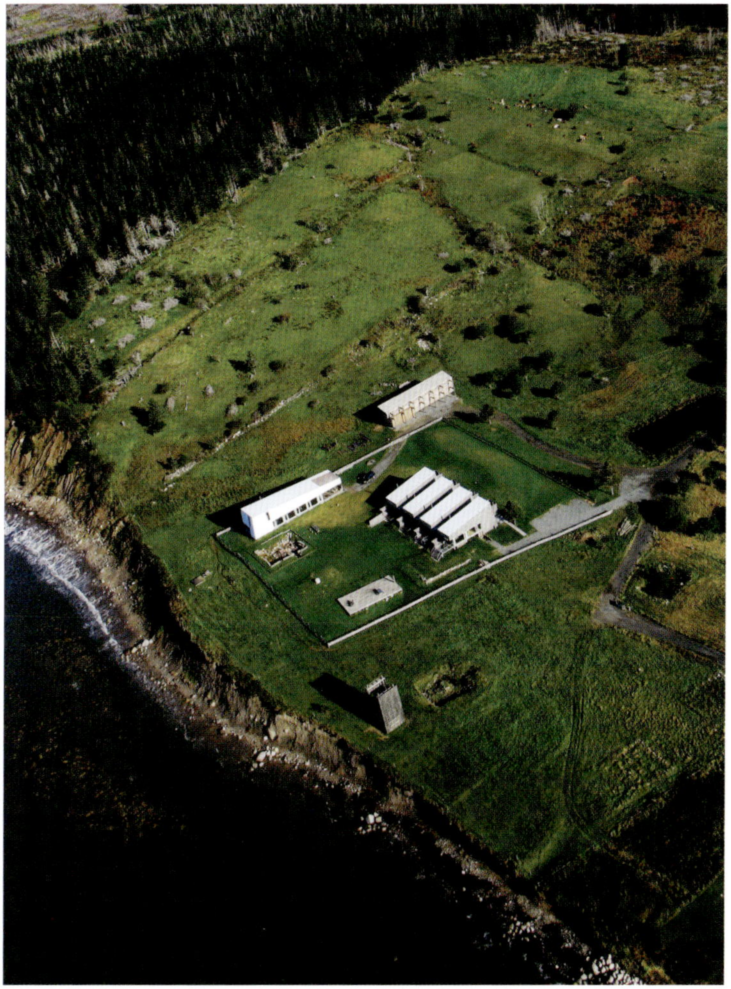

Pragmatism is the best teacher.
Learning is accelerated by purpose.
We learn best when we need to know.
Technology is best understood by making.
Teamwork is learned quickly when there is too much to do.

GHOST

Building an Architectural Vision
Brian MacKay-Lyons

With texts by
Peter Buchanan, Brian Carter, Thomas Fisher,
Kenneth Frampton, Karl Habermann, Robert Ivy,
Christine Macy, Robert McCarter, Juhani Pallasmaa

Princeton Architectural Press, New York

Published by
Princeton Architectural Press
37 East Seventh Street
New York, New York 10003

For a free catalog of books, call 1.800.722.6657.
Visit our website at www.papress.com.

© 2008 Princeton Architectural Press
All rights reserved
Printed and bound in China
11 10 09 08   4 3 2 1 First edition

No part of this book may be used or reproduced in any manner without written permission from the publisher, except in the context of reviews.

Every reasonable attempt has been made to identify owners of copyright. Errors or omissions will be corrected in subsequent editions.

Editor: Linda Lee
Acquisitions Editor: Nancy Eklund Later
Designers: Jan Haux and Deb Wood

Special thanks to: Nettie Aljian, Sara Bader, Dorothy Ball, Nicola Bednarek, Janet Behning, Becca Casbon, Penny (Yuen Pik) Chu, Russell Fernandez, Pete Fitzpatrick, Wendy Fuller, Clare Jacobson, Aileen Kwun, Laurie Manfra, Katharine Myers, Lauren Nelson Packard, Jennifer Thompson, Arnoud Verhaeghe, Paul Wagner, and Joseph Weston of Princeton Architectural Press
—Kevin C. Lippert, publisher

Library of Congress Cataloging-in-Publication Data

MacKay-Lyons, Brian.
Ghost : building an architectural vision / Brian MacKay-Lyons ; with essays by Peter Buchanan... [et al.].   p. cm.
ISBN 978-1-56898-736-1 (pbk. : alk. paper)
1. Ghost Lab. 2. Architecture—Study and teaching (Internship)—Nova Scotia. I. Buchanan, Peter. II. Title.
NA2130.N8M33 2008
720.71'509716—dc22
                              2007046651

Table of Contents

Preface / 10

Ghost 1   Ghost Stories by Christine Macy / 15
Hill / 35

Ghost 2   Concept and Construct/Earth and Sky by Brian Carter / 43
Landfall / 55

Ghost 3   Expedition to the Coast of Nova Scotia by Karl Habermann / 63
Pots and Pans / 73

Ghost 4   The Bones of Ghosts:
Structuring the Ephemeral by Robert Ivy / 81
Why Albert Oxner Shingled His Barn / 93

Ghost 5   On the Fringes of the Empire by Kenneth Frampton / 101
Barnyard / 111

Ghost 6   Seeing Ghosts by Thomas Fisher / 119
The Education of an Architect / 135

Ghost 7   The Dance of Construction by Juhani Pallasmaa / 143
Village Architect / 157

Ghost 8   Escaping Normality to Embrace Reality by Peter Buchanan / 165
Willing / 183

Ghost 9   The Thought of Construction by Robert McCarter / 191
Listening / 213

Contributor Biographies / 218
Ghost Participants / 220
Image Credits / 223
Acknowledgments / 224

Preface

The Ghost International Architectural Laboratory, better known as "Ghost Lab" or "Ghost," is the research laboratory of MacKay-Lyons Sweetapple Architects. The Ghost Lab began as a critique of architectural education in North America in the 1990s and represents an alternative to the current standard of practice. Ghost is rooted in the hands-on master-builder tradition, emphasizing an intimate interaction between master and apprentice in response to the increasingly virtual nature of architectural design. It focuses on timeless architectural themes of landscape, making, and community and provides a crash course in material culture through tangible, wooden constructions.

Nova Scotia is a lobster-shaped landmass off the eastern seaboard of North America hanging onto Canada by an isthmus. Arriving in Halifax, the capitol of Nova Scotia, one takes the scenic Lighthouse Route down the South Shore through Chester, Mahone Bay, and Lunenburg, a UNESCO World Heritage Site. Here the Ghost Lab takes place on a rural property overlooking the Atlantic Ocean. Buffered by sea breezes and ever-changing maritime weather, the site reflects the rugged beauty of the land and the determination and dedication of the people who have lived and worked it for over four hundred years.

In 1994, Brian MacKay-Lyons proposed a new spin on the Free Lab, a Dalhousie University course that pursues an architectural topic through hands-on work in a group format. Along with nine brave graduate students, MacKay-Lyons set up a two-week event on property he and his wife, Marilyn, owned on the South Shore of Nova Scotia, not far from Lunenburg. Housed in tents, with no washrooms or cooking facilities, the students and MacKay-Lyons set out to create something unique. Over the ruins of the previous settlements, the students, including Brian's now-partner Talbot Sweetapple, erected the first structure. A testament to simplicity, the structure mirrored an archetypal farmhouse—just a sparse wood frame, draped in white fabric. The structure was lit from inside: the entire building glowed like a ghost haunting the coast. It was the appearance of this initial structure that gave the program its name.

Each year's Ghost Lab revolves around a particular architectural research question. Over the past six years (Ghosts 4–9), guest architects and critics have been asked to participate. The addition of the guest architects and critics brought participants from other schools and practices willing to spend time learning and working with MacKay-Lyons and his colleagues.

Ghost is a two-week event: the first week is spent in designing the structure; the second in constructing. In addition to creating sketches, drawings, and models, the students meet with a structural engineer, Michel Comeau of Campbell Comeau Engineering, and the master builder, Gordon MacLean. Bob Benz of Thomas Anderson & Company also attends every year as a builder/architect. These guests are instrumental in bringing practicality to the event.

Once the design is finalized, the remainder of the time is spent building. Students learn the hands-on skills involved in erecting something from raw materials; from lumber and nails, extraordinary structures emerge. Plans often deviate from the original during the building process; participants learn the give-and-take of good design as the building rises from the ground.

The Ghost Lab has come a long way since 1994. From nine students and a professor from the Technical University of Nova Scotia (TUNS) roughing it in the near wilderness in its first year to thirty participants from schools and practices all across North America and Europe now living and working in permanent structures, Ghost Lab is an ever-evolving design-build event that promotes a tangible, poetic architecture of place.

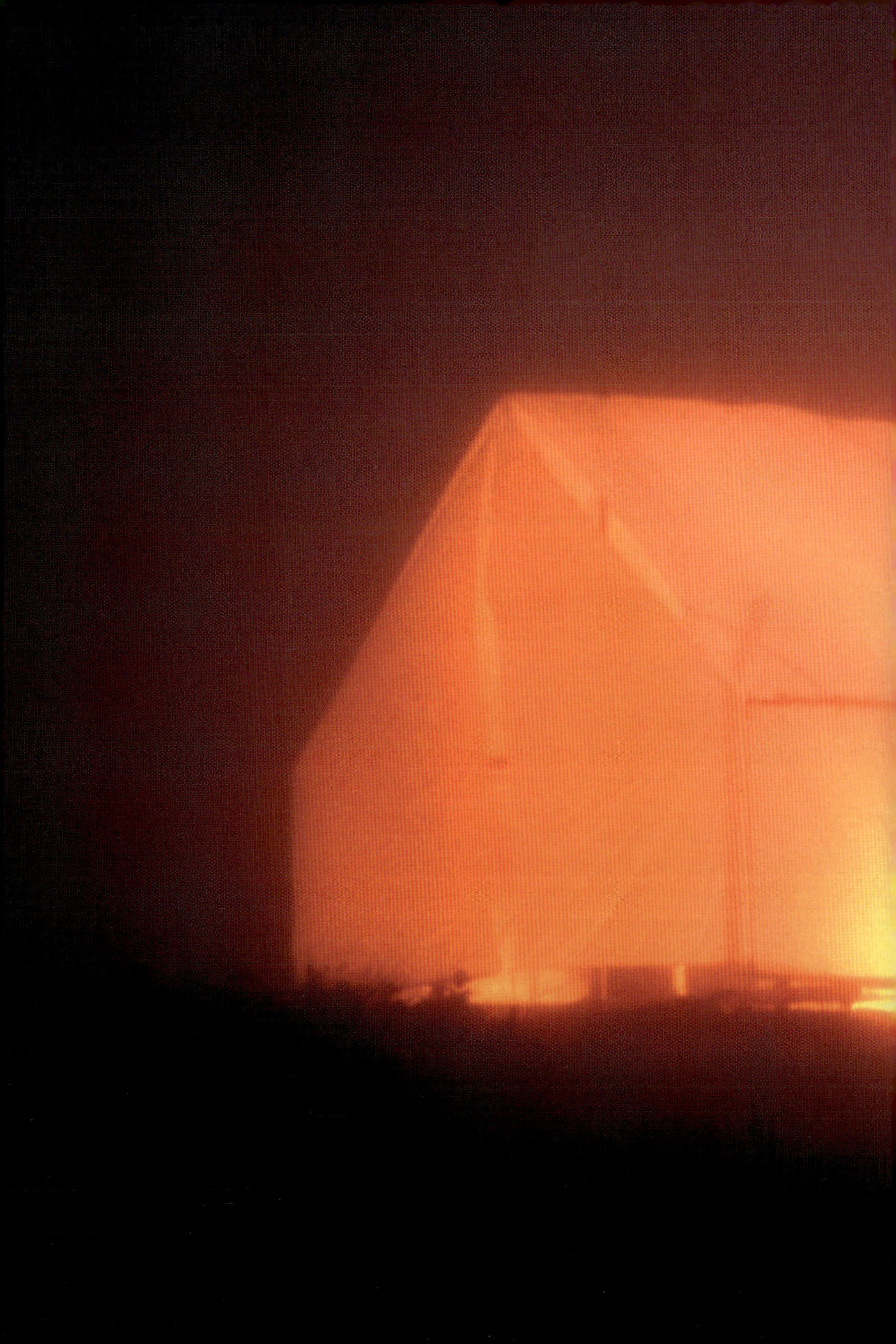

GHOST 1

May 2 to August 26, 1994

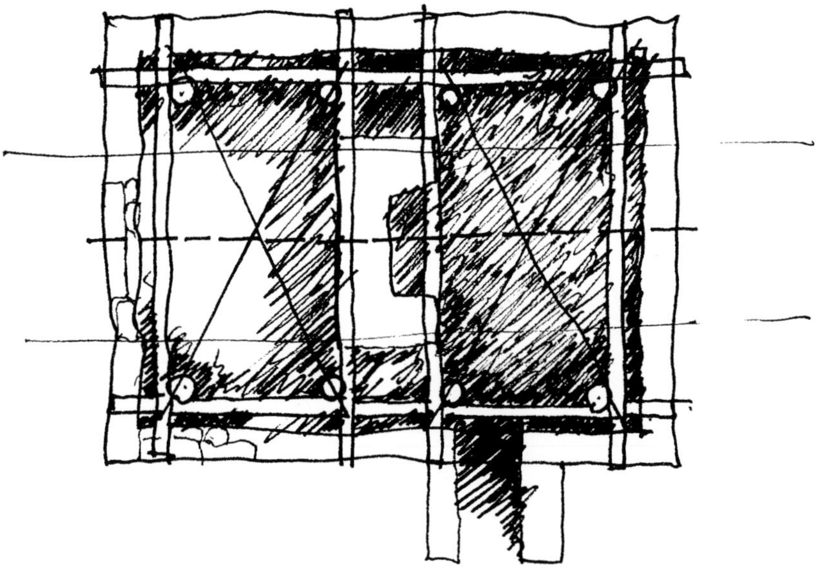

Ghost Stories

Christine Macy

For most of us, our first encounter with ghosts is through stories. We may remember parents or grandparents relating crucial events in the lives of ancestors, schoolteachers bringing to life forgotten figures from the past, or religious teachers revealing aspects of the spirit world. Riveting, evocative, at times terrifying, these stories allow us to feel and breathe the atmosphere of the past. We can imagine ourselves there. Ghost stories are a form of travel—not across space to other countries and cultures—but across time, carrying our imagination with us.

In the maritime provinces of Canada, stories from the past color all aspects of present-day life. As a native son of Nova Scotia, Brian MacKay-Lyons likes to tell stories—in person or through his projects. He anchors his buildings in local stories—the "vernacular" you might say. Whether the story is true or not is immaterial. MacKay-Lyons's tales, like good ghost stories, weave magic around the telling. They evoke a timeless culture and a landscape and allow the listener to project him- or herself into this imaginary ideal. As with fables and parables, such stories often carry a lesson.

"Close your eyes and imagine a foggy mid-summer's night. Imagine the glowing, translucent ghosts of archetypal buildings on the ruins of an abandoned village at the edge of the world."[1] This is MacKay-Lyons's evocation of Ghost, the first of a series of summer projects in the rural village of Upper Kingsburg on Nova Scotia's South Shore. In the first Ghost, nine architecture

---

I would like to thank Sarah Bonnemaison for her helpful suggestions and advice in the writing of this story.

1. Brian MacKay-Lyons, "Ghost: Seven Stories from a Village Architect," *Design Quarterly* 165 (Summer 1995): 20.

students set up camp on a ridge overlooking the "back forty" acres of MacKay-Lyons's summerhouse during the month of July. Before they even began the lab, the students had to set up their rudimentary spaces of social life and retreat—their sleeping area, cooking site, privy, and fire ring. Then they set to work.

The project site lay in the valley below their ridge encampment, a stone's throw from the ocean's edge. Their first task was to clear out the overgrowth, trash, and rubble that had filled the ruins of what once was a dwelling so that the outline of the old foundations could be clearly seen. Moving their efforts to the woods on the hill, they marked white spruce and pine trees of the desired diameter, chopped them down, and stripped them of their limbs and bark. They fashioned the timber into a "brace frame" over the old foundations, reconstructing the outline of a traditional one-and-a-half-story house with a gable roof—the kind found throughout the village, up the river, and over much of the province. The last task was to envelope the building skeleton in large sheets of plastic tarp to complete its exterior "walls."

The result was a resurrection of a house silhouette in a cow field—an apparition raised from earlier times. It could have been one of the earliest houses built along the LaHave estuary, like the ones Samuel de Champlain spotted in 1604 as he sailed up the river toward his first landfall on the North American continent. It could have been one of the sturdy houses erected by Dutch- and German-speaking settlers on land granted by the British in the 1750s. It could have been the ancestral seat of one of the established shipbuilding-fishing-farming families of nineteenth-century Nova Scotia. For local old-timers, it reminded them of the landscape of their youth and childhood.

On the final day of the lab, MacKay-Lyons and his students invited colleagues and classmates from Halifax, neighbors from all around, and local musicians to attend the closing event of Ghost. They, together with friends and passersby, converged in the night, drawn to the glowing profile of the reconstructed house. I was in one of the many small groups of people heading down the hill toward what was just a radiant glow at first, through the mist rising off the meadow as the night chill descended. As we drew nearer to the light, the profile of the house rose into relief—a lantern at a giant scale, its translucent wrapping distended with the heat rising off the roaring bonfire inside. We passed through an opening in the tarpaulin, where the door would have been in the original house, and found ourselves in a crowd of smiling faces bathed in firelight, sharing drinks and laughter while leaning against the battered boulders of the foundation. One group huddled around Judy Obersi, a student and master storyteller from Curaçao, who was sharing her grandmother's Caribbean ghost stories—closing the loop of maritime exchange between Europe, North America, and the West Indies with her Dutch and Creole stories.

This Ghost house, resurrected from the past, served as a conduit between history and story, memory and possibility. "I wanted to learn how to live at last," writes Jacques Derrida, by "being-with" ghosts. "It is necessary to speak *about* the ghost," he continues, "*to* the ghost and *with* it, as no ethics is possible without acknowledging respect for these others who are already dead or are not yet born."[2] By allowing a multitude of ghosts—"generations of ghosts"—to speak, we can break the domination of the present, open ourselves up to memory and heritage, and ultimately think about life beyond the present—toward survival of the larger culture and the world we live in. This essay looks at three "ghost stories" that MacKay-Lyons tells about Upper Kingsburg.

---

2. Jacques Derrida, *Specters of Marx*, trans. Peggy Kamuf (London: Routledge, 1994).

Champlain's Landfall

In 1604, the French explorer Samuel de Champlain took refuge in the river estuary he named La Have ("the Haven"). He mapped at that time a European-style house on what would eventually become our Ghost site.[3]

The first lesson is about home. When the expedition leader Pierre du Gua, sieur de Monts and his cartographer Champlain first saw a headland of the North American continent rising out of the Atlantic Ocean, they named it Cap de la Hève in memory of the last cape they passed in France before sailing across the sea.[4] Yet according to MacKay-Lyons's ghost story, the name was not just a fortuitous accident—it was a sign that this place was to become a safe *haven* for settling down: "Champlain was a cartographer, and the first drawing he made in the New World was of the LaHave estuary. It shows tepees and a few European houses. The story is that these were from an earlier Basque fishing camp."[5]

The next lesson is about traces. The few European houses are traces of earlier settlers, French, Basque, or Portuguese fishermen who decided to stay with the native Mi'kmaq people rather than return to Europe at the end of the fishing season, using the winter to collect valuable furs for trading with those who would return the following summer. According to Champlain in his *Voyages* published in 1605, "The people of Britanny, Normandy, and the Basque country were already frequenting the Great Banks of Newfoundland in 1504 and for a long time before that."

The European-style house then, drawn by Champlain on his map, was a house of an enterprising fisherman or his

---

3. MacKay-Lyons, "Ghost," 20.
4. Joan Dawson, "Historic LaHave River Valley: Images of Our Past," Fort Point Museum, http://www.fortpointmuseum.com/history.asp. Cap de la Hève, in the present-day French department of Seine-Maritime can be seen in Monet's painting *The Cape de la Hève at Low Tide*, 1865.
5. Brian MacKay-Lyons, conversation with the author, July 2007.

Root-cellar entrance

descendant, established long before the first official attempts at colonization and settlement. Champlain anchored only briefly at the mouth of the LaHave River before moving south to the Bay of Fundy, but while there he drew a chart of the river's mouth and the harbor. The act of tracing ("the first drawing he made in the New World") turns a ghost story into an architectural tale.

Before the digital age permeated the practice of architecture, architects used to speak of the "skeleton" or the "bones" of a building—these were the generating lines and structure of a work of architecture, traced lightly onto the fresh vellum. Layer after layer of drawing would "flesh it out," adding "skin" and systems, dimensions, and all the other information necessary for construction. Such drawings, created over months by many hands working on the same sheets, revealed shadows of earlier drawings that appeared on a sheet that had been worked over, erased, and reworked. These ghosts were memories, relics of bygone schemes—ancestors, if you will, of the building being finalized on the page. Today such ghosted drawings are only ghost stories, as each architectural drawing comes fresh from the plotter without visible trace of earlier schemes, or decisions, or changes of heart. Plotted sheets are unencumbered by memories of the past, yet in the design process, architects still use trace to carry one set of building studies forward into the next. In analyzing a site, they look at layers of habitation, seeing the cumulative traces of human settlement as a palimpsest of marks made on the surface of the earth, scraped clean with each successive wave of settlement to be made anew, yet carrying the faint records of earlier patterns. On the Ghost site, MacKay-Lyons works with exactly such traces, identifying the lines, residues, and marks of earlier buildings to anchor—or better, to root—his new works in this time-scarred landscape.

Two Neighbors and a Wall

Throughout the seventeenth and eighteenth centuries, French settlers peopled the shores of the LaHave River, living with the aboriginal Mi'kmaq in villages and encampments and carrying on fishing, furriering, forestry, and trade until the Acadian Expulsion in the mid-eighteenth century. The traces of this settlement and the one that followed lead us to the second ghost story of the site:

> After the expulsion of the Acadians, their farms and foundations in the LaHave drainage basin were occupied by German and Swiss settlers. These new settlers, in the 1750s, built a small farming and fishing village on our Ghost site at what seems like the end of the earth. This village, on a cliff over the beach, was a thriving place until the 1940s when it was abandoned. Now only the stone foundations of dozens of buildings remain. The extended family structure is evident: three houses, with three massive stone chimneys, next to three barns, six wells, three chicken houses, countless out buildings, twelve fish sheds. Why were these pragmatic pioneers concerned with classical order? Why did they take the trouble to align their houses, hearths, and wells on a north-south axis? This is a magical, silent place, where the ghost of a community can be felt.[6]

MacKay-Lyons adds in "Pots and Pans": "The village has four extended families: Moshers, Romkeys (Oxners), Mossmans, and Hirtles. Each family has three sons and so three houses."[7] Within these families people are placed in symmetrical relationships with each other: squared-off couplets of twos or fours or stable triangles of three sons in their houses. Geometry aligns these families with their land along north-south axes, east-west settlements, and radiating pinwheels that extend outward in

---

6. MacKay-Lyons, "Ghost," 21.
7. Brian MacKay-Lyons, "Pots and Pans," essay published in this volume.

Ghost 1

Ghost site, 1994

Raising a structural bent (left to right)

Ghost 1

Log frame

the landscape. At work, as MacKay-Lyons suggests, is a classical ordering system. The numbers come from the Renaissance architectural tradition of perfect geometries in which earthly and celestial patterns align. When earth and heavens are brought into congruence, through geometric arts such as architecture or dance, the earthly order manifests the perfection of the heavens. This is the belief system behind ideal cities of the Renaissance such as Filarete's Sforzinda. Although perfect geometries reflect an ideal that exists primarily in the mind, they have always exerted a steady gravitational pull on the imaginations of architects. Thus, we should not be surprised to find that the historical record of actual settlement is at odds with the idealized representation presented in the story. But it is not merely, as we shall soon see, a simple matter of truth versus fiction.

We find that the ancestors of the Mosher clan of Upper Kingsburg originated in Switzerland. Responding to the appeal of the British crown for European Protestants to settle in Canada, they descended the Rhine River to Rotterdam, where they boarded the *Speedwell* in the summer of 1751. In the years between 1750 and 1752, twelve shiploads of such "foreign Protestants" from Germany, Switzerland, and Holland arrived in Halifax—the result of an official policy to repopulate lands that had been evacuated of a hundred fifty years of French Acadian settlement. The blacksmith Jacob Moser and his wife, Anna Maria, embarked on the journey with their children, a nearly grown daughter and four younger boys. After arriving in Halifax, they were assigned two lots and a one-hundred-acre tract in Upper Kingsburg. They had more children after arriving in the New World, and in 1764, Mrs. Moser was working as a midwife in the growing town of Lunenburg. The same boat also brought Peter Moser, who may have been a brother of Jacob, since kin often traveled together.

Ghost 1

The *Speedwell* carried no passenger with the name Romkey. But a likely candidate is Johann Wendel Ramichen who, in his middle age, departed from Rotterdam for Halifax aboard the *Ann* in 1750 with his wife, Anna Margaretha Uhrig, and their grown children, Ursela (who died shortly after arrival), Anna Maria, Conrad, and Anna. In the German Palatinate on the Rhine River, Wendel had been a master linenweaver. The family spent three winters in Halifax before moving to Lunenburg, eventually settling at a hamlet called Five Houses on the LaHave River where Anna Margaretha's brother, Leonard Uhrig, had been assigned a thirty-acre farm lot. In the eight generations between their arrival in Nova Scotia and the close of this ghost story, the family name gradually anglicized into Romkey.

Neither the Moshers nor the Romkeys had sons in threes. The descendants of Jacob and Anna Maria Moser typically had ten or more children up to the end of the nineteenth century, when much smaller families became the norm. The Ramichen's only son, Conrad, also finally settled down in Five Houses, and of his eleven children that survived to adulthood, the six boys averaged eight children apiece, and the five daughters married into other families, distributing relatives all through the lower LaHave River basin, including the communities of Riverport, Kingsburg, and Rose Bay.

In her influential book *Fiction in the Archives*, the historian Natalie Zemon Davis explores how "historical" stories are actually shaped for their purposes, reflecting the literary tastes and cultural strategies of their tellers. The fiction in history refers to the craft that goes into stories—the fabrication, we might say. To navigate the frontier between truth and fiction—for that matter, to understand and appreciate a story at all—one must "consider the genre in which the person is writing [or speaking and] the

---

8. Natalie Zemon Davis, "A Life of Learning" (Charles Homer Haskins Lecture for 1997, American Council of Learned Societies, Occasional Paper No. 39, 1997). See also, Zemon Davis, *Fiction in the Archives: Pardon Tales and Their Tellers in Sixteenth-Century France* (Palo Alto, CA: Stanford University Press, 1990).

Ghost 1

Trimming the sails

Log-to-cable connection

Raising the ridge beam

conventions he or she is expected to follow."⁸ Thus, as MacKay-Lyons hears stories, takes them in, and retells them in his own way, he crafts them to architectural ends. If they were preserved instead of being retold, they would merely be records from the past, neither heard nor really understood. Once again, we turn to Derrida, who, in the film *Ghost Dance*, talks about how ghost stories help us to make the past part of the present, to accept it and our place in relation to it.

> I've been intrigued by a particular theory [of ghosts], which psychoanalyst friends of mine…developed from Freud. In normal mourning, says Freud, one internalizes the dead. One takes the dead into oneself, and assimilates them. This internalization (which is at the same time an idealization) accepts the dead. In a mourning that doesn't develop naturally [according to this theory], the dead are taken into us but don't become a part of us. They just occupy a place in our bodies. They haunt our bodies and ventriloquize our speech…and we become a sort of graveyard for ghosts.⁹

If we try to preserve the past as it was rather than accept it as a memory, we cannot fully understand it or apply it to the present. The stories we tell about the past may be part of a tradition yet still our own. This is because, Zemon Davis suggests, traditions are "ways of thinking, doing, and feeling" that we inherit from the past. There is no such thing as a "true" or "authentic" tradition, she suggests. Rather, tradition is made of many voices and within tradition: "there can be different paths and room even to find something new while perhaps labeling it traditional. Innovations that expand the boundaries or redraw them in a different shape usually take something from what went before."¹⁰ This is what MacKay-Lyons is trying to do with his contemporary

---

9. Jacques Derrida in Ken McMullen's *Ghost Dance* (London: Channel Four Films, 1983), filmstrip.
10. Violeta Davoliute, "Babel is Not the Last Word: A Conversation with Natalie Zemon Davis," *Eurozine*, http://www.eurozine.com/articles/2005-07-28-zemondavis-en.html.

Ghost 1

Christine Macy and Dalhousie students

Albert and Beulah Oxner
on their wedding day

"regional" architecture in Nova Scotia, anchoring it in a tradition while accepting his own voice, his memories, and his interpretations of the place as valid parts of that tradition.

Beulah's Memories in the Cellar and the Attic

Although the Romkey clan was anchored in Five Houses, they had relations all across the LaHave region. By the fourth generation (mid-nineteenth century), one Romkey cousin—a John Leonard Romkey, to be precise—settled with his wife, Maria, to farm in Upper Kingsburg, where they had three girls and a son, Henry. Henry was widowed early, and in middle age he remarried again, to Drusilla Oxner, a forty-year-old spinster from Lower LaHave. Of their two daughters, the elder, Selena, married Ambrose Oxner, who moved in with the family in Upper Kingsburg. The county census of 1911 describes the household: thirty-eight-year-old Ambrose Oxner (now officially head of the family) and his wife, Selena; their three older daughters, Helen, Bessie, and Maggie; and three younger sons, Albert, Harry, and William. They lived with Selena's elderly parents, Henry and Drusilla Romkey. The Oxners' middle child and their oldest son, Albert, married Beulah Mae Zinck, taking us to our third, and last, ghost story.

> This story is about the matriarch of the community, my neighbor Beulah Oxner. She was an orphan—her mother died when she was young, and her father, rather than raise her, put her out to work as a domestic in the community. She lived in the basement of the original Mosher home (where we built the first Ghost), putting up sausages, preserves, pickles, and Solomon Gundy [pickled herring]. Albert Oxner, whose father married into the Romkey family, had cattle, which he pastured near the river not far from the Mosher home. He and Beulah courted and got married, and she moved into the Romkey house up the hill. Once she had set up a household of her own, her

---

11. MacKay-Lyons, conversation with author, July 2007.

father moved back in with her. The basement of Ghost was the place where she had worked as a young girl, in the house that used to be there.[11]

This story is about family lost and gained and the difference between house and home. Beulah Oxner was born a Zinck, and her family had been established in Rose Bay since the eighteenth century. In one of that village's cemeteries, a headstone tells us that Laura Hilda Zinck, wife of James Zinck, died in late 1918—the year of the massive influenza epidemic—at twenty-four years of age. She left behind the three-year-old Beulah Mae and a brother, Allen, who had to be cared for by female relatives of the young widower, at least until the children were old enough to be put to work. Thus, the excavated foundations of Ghost brought up memories of hardship as well.

Beulah's memories in the cellars and attics of Upper Kingsburg were triggered by spaces she had experienced long ago. They were summoned up through her senses and the landscape: the sound of wind through the grass, the light playing off waves in the tidal river, and the smell of sea air. And of course, her age gave her a vast store of memories to draw from, as she told stories about her landscape to MacKay-Lyons and his students working on Ghost.

Ghosts such as these—memories and architecture—weave the past into the present, giving meaning and continuity to actions in the here and now.

Ghost 1

The morning after

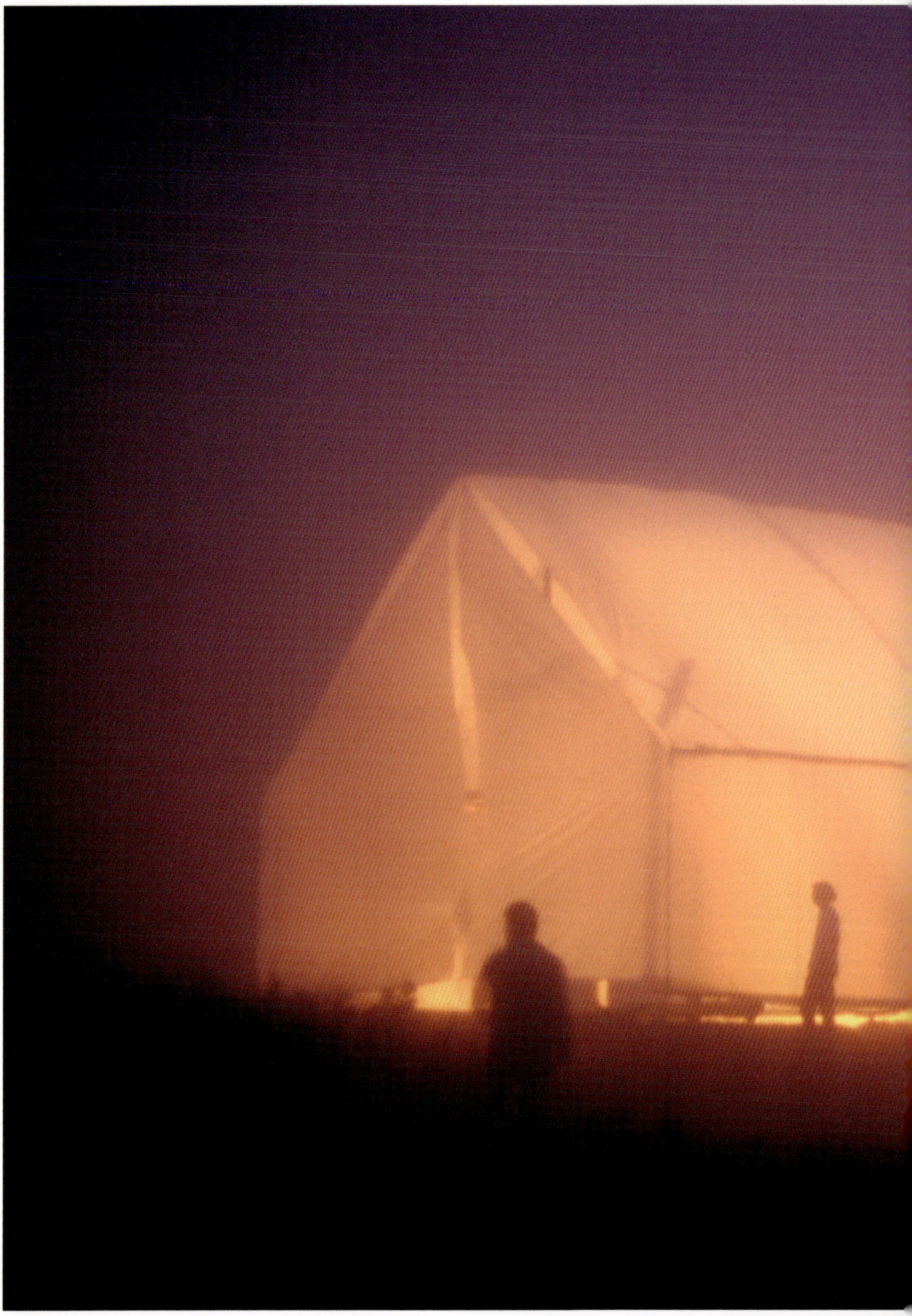

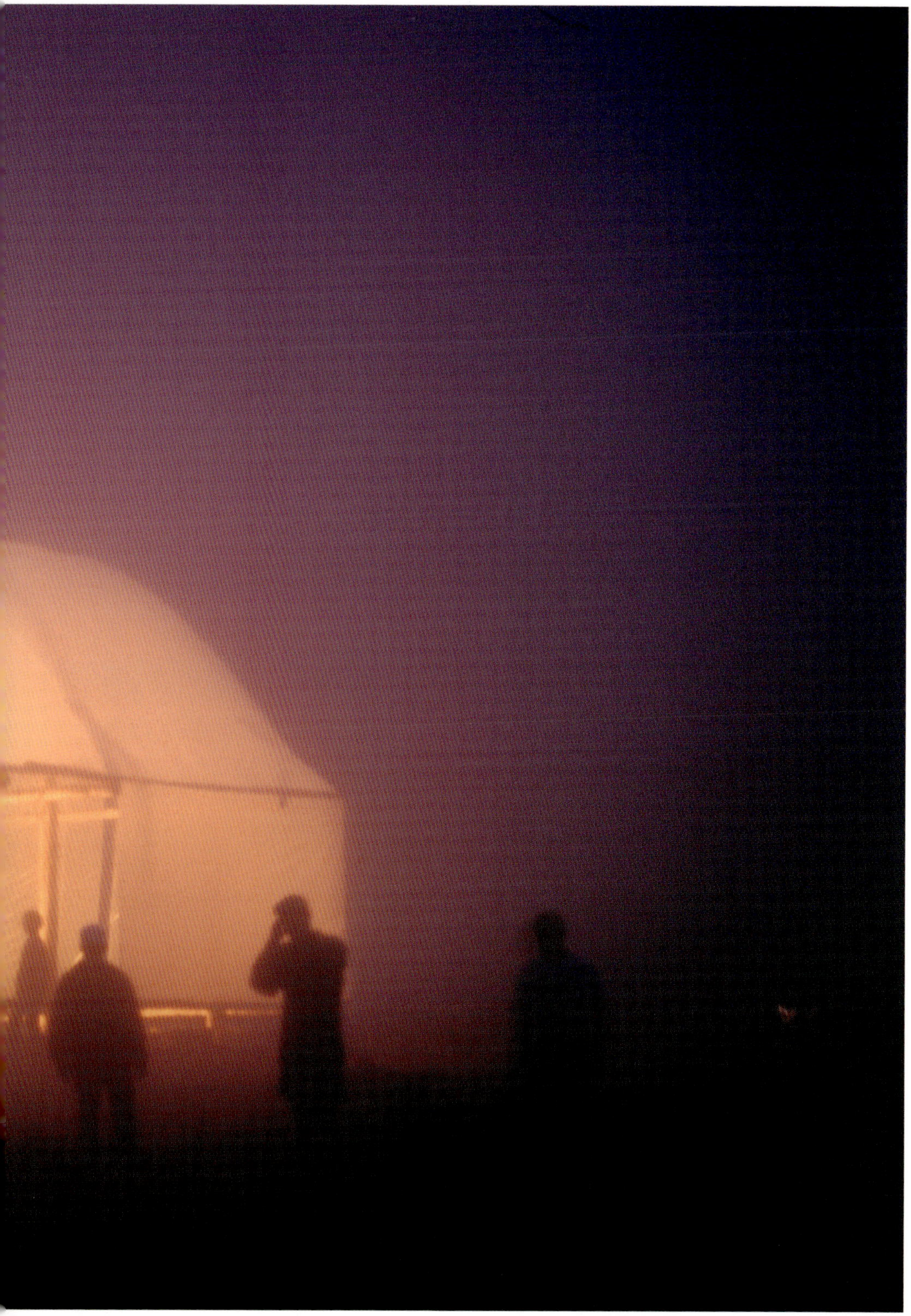

Ghost site, circa 1900

Hill

I wanted it to be all the hills, and yet a very definite hill.
—Andrew Wyeth

During the last ice age, about fifteen thousand years ago—just the day before yesterday in geological time—the landscape of the "ghost village" was shaped by glacier movement. The advancing glacier ploughed the land flat, down to the sedimentary, shale bedrock, while picking up and transporting stones and soil the way a child incorporates schoolyard gravel into a rolled snowball. The retreating glacier deposited the debris from hundreds of miles away in long, lozengelike piles on the northwest axis of the retreat, perpendicular to the Nova Scotian coast. The result is a county distinguished by its parallel glacial hills, or drumlins, containing a combination of rich topsoil and a variety of foreign granite stones smoothed by thousands of years of tumbling within the glacier. The pattern laid down by the glaciers is like a musical staff over which the melody of human settlement has been laid, ultimately producing the genius loci, or particular sense of place, for this region, from the scale of the landscape to the scale of pots and pans, from architectural time to geological time.

When this drumlin landscape touches the coast—as in the case of our ghost village—a rich set of conditions arise. At the coastline the loamy drumlins dissolve into the sea like salt or sugar, forming the cliffs or conspicuous banks referred to in nautical charts and used as landmarks by sailors. Drumlins that landed in the sea are many of the rounded agrarian islands that dot Mahone Bay. Drumlins are eroded both from their base, due to undermining wave-and-storm tidal-surge action, and from the cliff tops, due to a combination of dugout bird homes and the groundwater that bleeds out of the face. In an ongoing circle of loss and gain, the eroding soil is washed out to sea each winter. The organic material contained within the soil rots out. What remains is sand that redeposits in summer, feeding the beaches. These beaches have been built up over centuries on ridges formed by windrows of rounded granite stones that have long since rolled out of the retreating drumlins. The ocean inlets between the drumlins are therefore blocked off from the sea, forming freshwater lakes, which are fed by runoff water from the drumlins. Freshwater fishing is carried out in the lakes behind the beaches while saltwater fishing is carried out on the sea in front of the beaches. The ghost village has three beaches, five lakes, and six drumlins. The LaHave Islands dot the horizon offshore.

These landforms produce a particular kind of subsistence agrarian pattern that combines offshore fishing, farming on loamy drumlins, and forestry on the less fertile, shaley hills. Roads follow the geomorphology of the land, running parallel to the long, gently sloping northwest axis of the drumlins. (The Old Northwest Road—through the village of Northwest—was the first road laid out by British colonial navy surveyors and forms the baseline for all other roads in the county.) Every drumlin has a hauling road along its northwest axis, which takes advantage of the relatively gentle slope on this long axis of the hill. Every drumlin has a series of dug wells, which follows a seam of gravel where the water table bleeds out the side of the hill. Farms are small because the drumlins are small, and the lowlands between them are rocky, wet, and acidic. The aesthetic result is a perky, small-scaled landscape. Even small changes in built form or land use have a large impact on this fragile ecology.

Architecture must begin with the land. The historic agrarian patterns of settlement were clear and sustainable; arable land was conserved, and buildings did not consume valuable farmland. The newer recreational patterns are consumptive: they occupy the center of the site, interrupting the continuity of the fields and making agriculture unfeasible. As simple farmhouses and barns gradually lay down and die, they are replaced by alien holiday homes whose owners and designers show little understanding of the language of the place. The truth, however, is that these buildings, like their predecessors, will one day also disappear. Like the dissolving drumlins, all signs of human habitation are little more than a thin layer of mold on the surface of the earth in the face of the powerful processes of nature. The idea of permanence is the vanity of man.

The projects of the Ghost Lab respond to a particular sense of place, based on local ecology, and its specific material culture, based on a subsistence agrarian economy. In all disciplines one can only arrive at universal principles through focus on the particular. There is no shortcut. French impressionist painter Claude Monet painted the waterlilies in his own garden again and again—they revealed not only his backyard, but the world. English language theorist Northrop Frye argued in *The Great Code: The Bible and Literature* (Harcourt & Brace Jovanovich, 1982) that Shakespeare invented no new stories. All the stories and the great themes in art and literature already exist, waiting to be rediscovered. As Goethe writes in "Gott, Gemütt und Welt" (1918): "If in the infinite you want to stride, just walk the finite to every side."

The Ghost Lab projects are built responses to the cultural ecology of a particular place and make an argument for an ecological way of building everywhere. Likewise, the community concerts, which celebrate the completion of each Ghost Lab, are specific occasions on specific nights, each with unique weather conditions (e.g., calm, full moon, fog, etc.), but they also approach the idea of timeless rituals of community. Many maritime cultures have their own version of ghost stories. Even B-grade horror films tell of the night when crypts open, and the souls of the dead ancestors walk again among us. The power of the Ghost Lab constructions derives in part from the fact that while they are extremely temporary and ephemeral, they are also extremely archetypal and ancient (e.g., burning ships, burning tower, burning house of maritime stories). They are for one night, and for all time.

Ghost 1

Ghost site, circa 1960

GHOST 2

July 1 to July 30, 1995

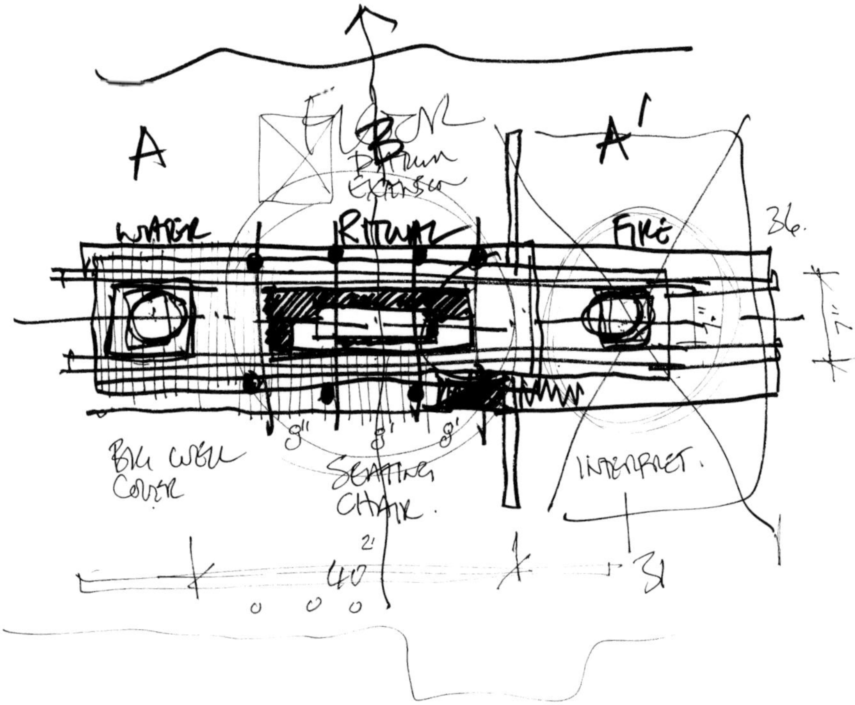
A
A'
RITUAL
FIRE
36.
8'
8'
8'
2'
40

Concept and Construct/ Earth and Sky

Brian Carter

ghost / n 1 supposed apparition of a dead person or animal; disembodied spirit 2 shadow or semblance 3 secondary optical image or blur

Prompted by the discovery of a small excavated basement on a headland overlooking the Atlantic Ocean, a group of architects and students made the site in Nova Scotia a focus of study and celebration. Their subsequent investigations were to reveal centuries of fitful occupation on this remote landfall at the northeastern edge of North America and to eventually inspire an energetic reoccupation of the place.

In 1994, Ghost created an ancient house, which reappeared briefly like an apparition—and then it was gone. This ghost and the place of its appearance were to become the basis for a sustained and innovative educational program. The program adopted this haunted site as the setting for regular expeditions, systematic research, and annual design workshops.

The presence of the remains of this particular primitive hut having already been registered, the students who traveled to Upper Kingsburg a year later sought to expand understandings of the tiny constructed space in a broader context. Looking beyond the confines of the stone basement, Ghost 2 focused on the creation of a device that would connect the built fragment to its site and the landscape beyond. Designed as a long, narrow horizontal platform, this device was centered on the existing basement and bridged across the space defined by the retaining walls that marked the outline of the house. The ninety-six-foot-long framed structure, lifted up off the ground and conspicuously light, was a stark contrast to the massive stone basement walls and excavated ground. The platform also extended across the site and around an existing well before dropping down a broad flight of steps that was suspended above the rough grass. Conceived as a primitive surveying tool, the platform located the house and referenced the rise and fall of the land around it while at the same time providing a datum against which to view the undulating headland, the expansive flatness of the ocean, and the distant horizon.

In seeking to look beyond the confines of an individual building and consider the potential of architecture in the service of science, the construction of this strange device brings to mind other built instruments. As the carefully carved and precisely assembled blocks at Stonehenge provided a unique place for individuals to gather and register their place in the world, centuries later the precise instrumentation developed by Jai Singh II created an unlikely global positioning system at Jantar Mantar. Created from stones precisely marked with graded measures, these strikingly abstract structures were shaped by people anxious to understand the place they occupied. The three-dimensional forms that they built established enduring connections between concept and construct, earth and sky.

Located alongside the royal palace on the outskirts of New Delhi in India, the instruments at Jantar Mantar were developed from a series of large-scale mockups. First assembled on smooth, flat constructed platforms of stone, the design of the structures was refined in an iterative process that extended over several years before the completion of an extensive group of small buildings in 1727—an impressive collection that still exists

Ghost 2

Beach classroom

Hearth restoration

Precedent, Snyder's Shipyard

today. The device at Upper Kingsburg was built by a team of people who worked in a similar way. Design and construction ran in parallel, ideas were tested by building on-site at full scale, and details were modified and improved throughout the construction. However, the work in Nova Scotia was completed in a few weeks—a constraint created in part by the routine of the academic calendar but one which also recalled the intense activity of the first settlers who, arriving at this remote place, had to work quickly and ingeniously with few resources to create shelter within the strict sequence of the seasons.

At Upper Kingsburg, wood replaces the stones of Stonehenge and Jantar Mantar. A readily available material that is easily worked, its use was enriched by long-established traditions of building in this region. In Nova Scotia, wood has also been used for many years to make boats—sophisticated instruments that were tested regularly by use and the elements. While both wood and stone can be carved, this recent constructional experiment sought to explore those vernacular traditions alongside the potential of the structural frame and the liberating orders of tectonic construction.

Aware of the remoteness of the place and the challenges faced by the original builders, the students engaged in Ghost 2 also worked with a modest and finite supply of material. Presented with four hundred and ninety-five pieces of rough-cut two-by-four lumber, these designer-builders planned a platform supported on two specially fabricated timber beams that spanned between nine pairs of circular wooden posts cut from tree trunks and driven into the ground at twelve-foot centers. Acknowledging the lack of plentiful, sophisticated fasteners as another constraint that the first builders had to contend with, the team for this project was supplied with just one hundred and fifty pounds of four-inch common nails. To further underline the value and potential of this simple connector that had once been such a precious commodity but is now ubiquitous, the team focused their work by devising construction systems that used those nails only in shear.

Like the original house, this new instrument was built with few tools, a minimal amount of equipment, and by effectively engaging the human body. Consequently, the large structure was made of relatively small pieces that could be easily worked, conveniently handled, simply connected, and efficiently assembled by a small group of people.

In addition to being a primitive scientific device and a constructional experiment, this new platform was also envisaged as a lookout to survey the site and re-view the land. It offered a series of new vantage points and identified places of significance within the stone walls of the rediscovered basement. A cutout at the northern end of the platform located the central chimney of the ancient house and signaled the hearth—a place with obvious domestic associations but which also plays a civic role that arises out of the gathering together of people and conversations around the fire.[1] While that hearth can be seen as an inseparable part of the earthwork, the contrasting tectonic frame of the new wooden deck elevated above the stone-walled basement clearly recalled both the construction systems of the original house and the architectural treatises of Gottfried Semper. In addition to restoring a partial floor to the house and focusing upon the hearth, the platform also extended out across the site to define the well with a second cutout so as to connect fire and water. It terminated in a new stair that hovered tenuously above the ground. In this way the platform celebrated the sequence of entry into the house but also underlined that all-important

---

1. Kenneth Frampton, *Studies in Tectonic Culture* (Cambridge, MA: MIT Press, 1995), 86.

Ghost 2

Colonnade

Cariatids

Table base

48

civilizing moment when the first settlers moved up off the ground to make a better life.

A rudimentary ædicule was constructed on the platform in the space between house and well. As if to further emphasize the distinction between the stereotomic earthwork and the tectonic frame of the primordial house, it also created a place for the new settlers of Upper Kingsburg to gather alongside the spaces that had been occupied by their predecessors. In this way, the platform became a stage for a thirty-foot totemic banquet table where the rituals of domesticity could again be acted out.

Ghost 2 created the first of a series of instruments to be constructed on the site at Upper Kingsburg. That particular device, well used during the time it was being designed and built, was subsequently dismantled and the materials reused to realize other experimental projects. Like the original house, the project is now a memory. However, it, and the investigations that followed, was vital in providing better understanding of the site and deeper appreciation of the nature of building in this place.

Simultaneously, other forces were also reshaping the economic landscape of the maritimes; increases in tourism and the consequent reoccupation of the land are introducing another life to Nova Scotia. In this changing context, the studies initiated by Ghost were eventually to lead to the sensitive reuse of the land. New housing has been built as a result of the energy, curiosity, and discoveries of those first initiatives, and the disembodied spirits released from that solitary excavation have inspired the founding of alternative communities at this edge of the world.

Long beams

Surveying instrument

Ghost 2

Curious neighbors

Finger-jointed stair

Team photo

Ghost 2

Lean-to

Ghost 2

Typical shear connection

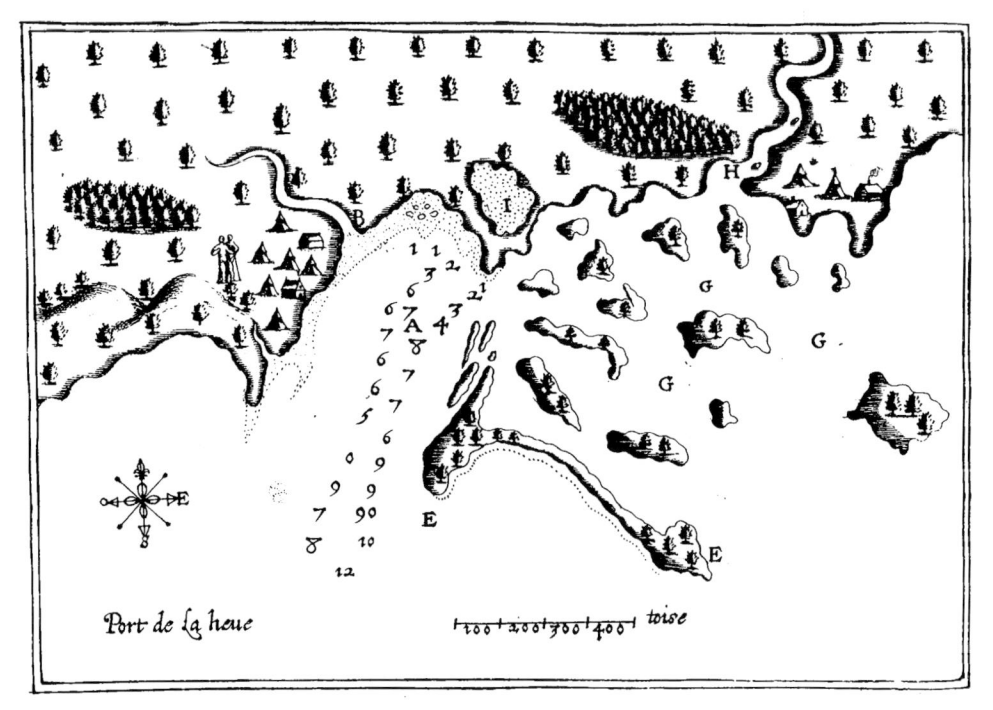

Champlain's map

Landfall

This is the forest primeval. The murmuring pines and the Hemlocks,
Bearded with moss, and in garments green, indistinct in the twilight,
Stand like Druids of eld, with voices sad and prophetic,
Stand like harpers hoar, with beards that rest on their bosoms.
Loud from its rocky caverns, the deep-voiced neighbouring ocean
Speaks, and in accents disconsolate answers the wail of the forest.
—Henry Wadsworth Longfellow, "Evangeline: A Tale of Acadie"

In 1604, French explorer and cartographer Samuel de Champlain set out from France on his second voyage to the New World in the party of Pierre du Gua, sieur de Monts. His first landfall of the voyage was at the estuary of what is now called the LaHave River, which he named after Cap de la Hève, the last headland passed on departing France. The first of his famous series of maps of the New World, drawn in 1604, documents the LaHave River mouth, the LaHave Islands, and what is now the Ghost site. The pictomap indicates aboriginal wigwams and what appears to be a European house, complete with gabled roof, chimney, and windows on the western shore of the Kingsburg Peninsula. Whether this structure was built by earlier Basque or French fishermen visiting these shores is not certain. The first Ghost in 1994 was built on this foundation.

Sieur de Monts and Champlain subsequently founded the habitation at Port Royal—near present-day Annapolis Royal—the first official, permanent European settlement in North

America north of St. Augustine in Florida and the beginning of the colony of Acadia (*l'Acadie*). *Acadie* is the native Mi'kmaq, the indigenous people of the region, word for a tidal marshland with a rich and diverse ecosystem. It is the name given by the aboriginal people to the early French settlers (Acadians) who typically settled on these marshlands, intermarried with the natives, and formed a new and distinctive culture—the culture of my mother, Jeanette Marie d'Entremont.

    The Ghost site was, long ago, where the Mi'kmaq resided during the summer. During the 1600s and 1700s, it was part of the Acadian settlement at LaHave. During the 1630s, LaHave housed the capitol of New France, at Fort St. Marie de Grace. In 1755, the British carried out the expulsion of the peaceful Acadians ("Le Grand Derangement"), scattering them far and wide. This bit of demographic engineering is one of the most brutal passages in British colonial history and is mythologized in Henry Wadsworth Longfellow's epic poem "Evangeline" (1893). Many avoided exile by hiding in the woods with their Mi'kmaq cousins. Of those expelled, some created non-French settlements and culture in North America and beyond, most notably the Cajuns in Louisiana. Most (or their children) returned to Acadia within twenty-five years. The story of their journey back by ox cart is told in *Pélagie-la-Charette* (Grasset, 1979) by Antonine Maillet. "Ghosts" of this Acadian period are visible today in several place names in the ghost village: Old House Road and Old Cellar, for example, are how Acadian foundation ruins are referred to by later settlers.

    In this part of Nova Scotia, a majority of the surviving buildings, agrarian landscape patterns, and artifacts are the legacy of "foreign Protestants" from Germany, Switzerland, and France, who occupied the land following the expulsion of the Acadians in the 1750s. Their ghost village began as an agrarian settlement, was joined by inshore fishery and forestry, and later connected to the development of the Grand Banks deep-sea fishery.

Each historic layer of settlement on the Ghost site is built atop the previous layer, reusing its precious foundation stones. Each new people recognized the same merits of the site that the aboriginals did—fertile soils, anchorage, protective microclimate. The large granite boulders, worn round by the glaciers and found in the forested hills surrounding the valley of the Ghost site, were hand-split to make square foundation stones. Children would drill a line of approximately four-inch-deep holes in the hard boulder by tedious tapping and rotating of an iron chisel. Then five or six metal wedges called "feathers" would be driven into each of the holes. A fire would be lit to heat the stone, followed by dousing the heated rock with cold water to facilitate the splitting. The split stones would then be dragged to the construction site on a sled drawn by oxen and then lifted into position.

These massive foundations were not often structurally sound, due to a lack of knowledge by the new European settlers of the local climate and its wet/dry, freeze/thaw cycles. Hydrostatic pressure usually pushed the foundations inward into the basements, especially after the wooden house above, which provided ballast, had rotted away. It is not surprising, given the tremendous investment in manufacturing foundations, that each subsequent culture rebuilt using the same stones. The result is both a transitory and a permanent architecture—the Ghost site carries the memory of many centuries of tenuous, fitful inhabitation.

The habitation constructed at Port Royal remains a powerful archetype within Canadian culture. Its pure, irreducible courtyard conveys the very essence of the ideal refuge. This early mark on the landscape is an expression of the precarious nature of human inhabitation on a vast and sparsely populated land. In Canada, the cultural mythology is greatly rooted in the relative insignificance of man against a big and dangerous Nature. Canadians are first hunters and gatherers rather than farmers; we began as *couriers du bois*, voyageurs, fur traders, fishermen, and, even today, our economy is based on primary-resource extraction. The memory of Champlain's habitation is the model for the courtyard at the Ghost site. Unlike its historic predecessor, the Ghost court is more porous and less defensive in character. The gaps between the buildings allow the meadow grass and the ocean views to flow through and connect to the islands of the LaHave River estuary and to the horizon beyond.

In recent years the agrarian culture of this place has declined and been erased and replaced by a new layer of "come-from-aways," who seek to exploit this beautiful landscape for recreational, rather than productive, purposes. These are largely seasonal residents from far and wide, in search of sanctuary from the stresses of a fast-paced modern existence, as explored in Larry Gaudet's *Safe Haven: The Possibility of Sanctuary in an Unsafe World* (Random House Canada, 2007). Ironically, in order to relax, they must be connected by wireless internet to the world that they seek to escape.

At the annual community concert, musicians play out the layers of inhabitation through songs of their aboriginal, Acadian, German, Irish, and Scottish ancestry. The drone of the bagpipes summons the community at dusk and the ghosts of those who have lived on this site.

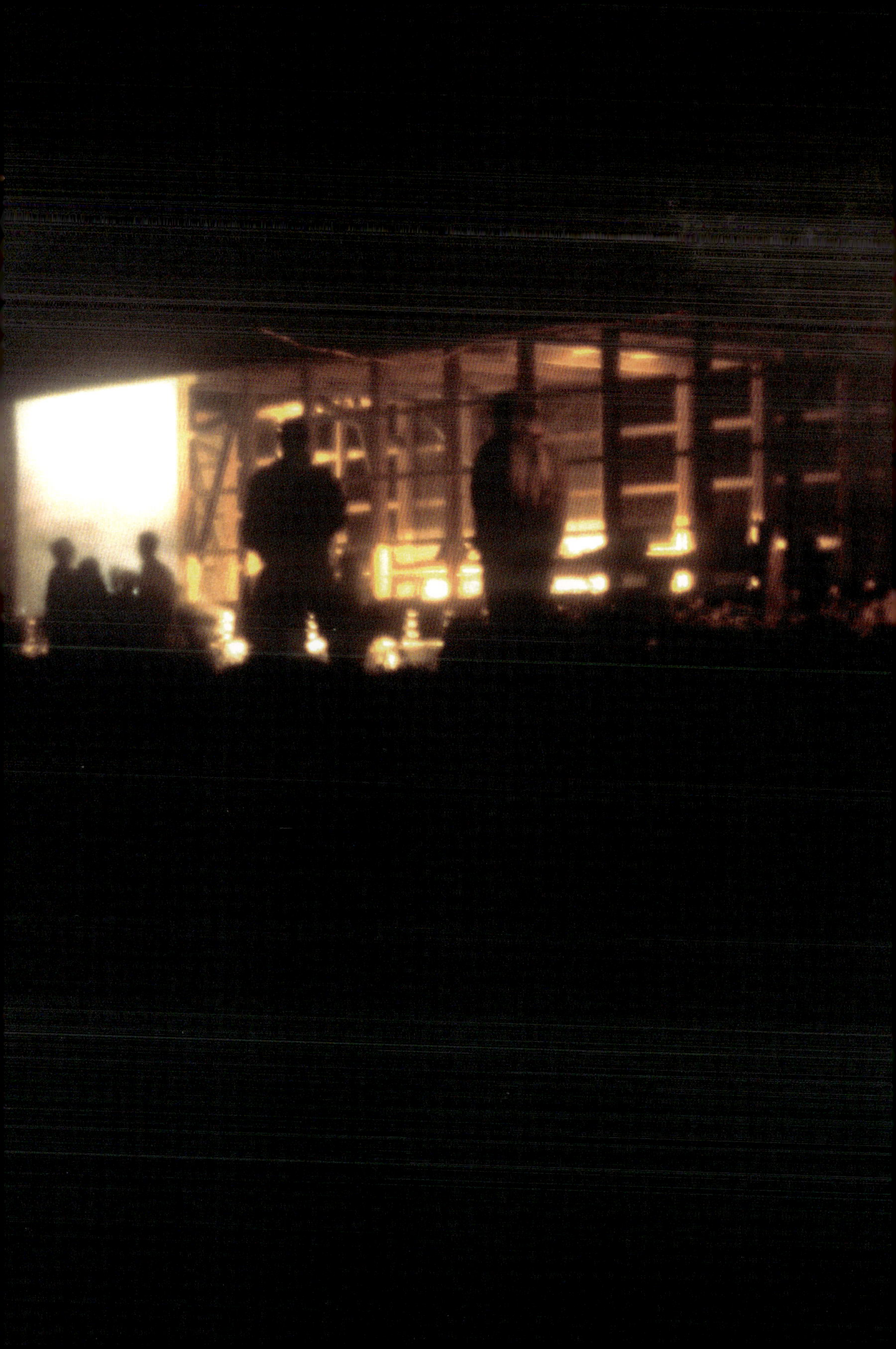

GHOST 3

June 28 to July 27, 1997

NO DEAD ENDS

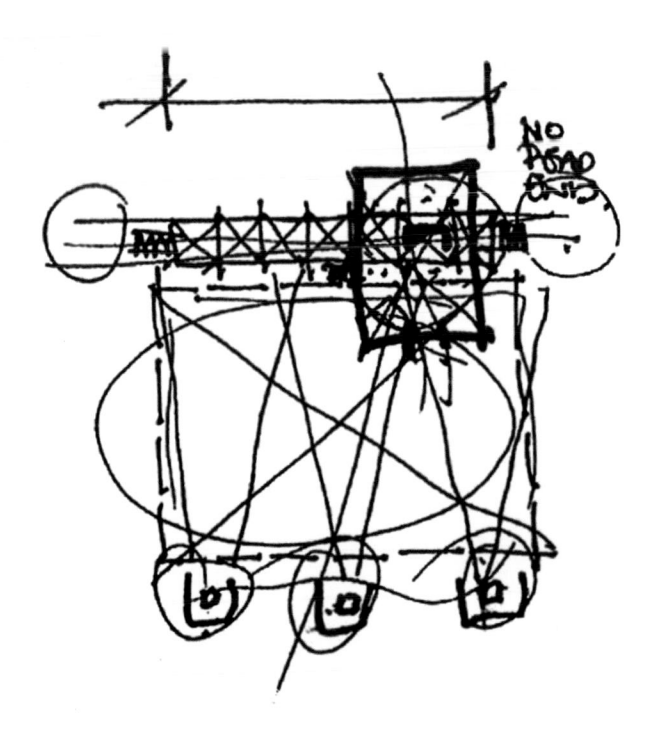

Expedition to the Coast of Nova Scotia

Karl Habermann

I arrived in Nova Scotia and embarked on a journey that led me through the myths of the development of the Nova Scotia landscape. Here, in miniature, was the territorial conquest of America by the immigrants from Europe. Agriculture and fishing were the lifeblood of the settlers, many of whom had emigrated to avoid persecution for their beliefs or to leave poverty behind. The building culture, based upon the naturally available wood resources, led people with diverse cultural roots to become a single community. Shipbuilding and construction were practiced by the same craftsmen. As a result, one finds constructional parallels and formal cross references everywhere.

A grasp of the vernacular characteristics of the native building culture leads to an understanding of current building styles. Why do the buildings from the Ghost workshop blend so well with the existing landscape? It is because Brian MacKay-Lyons has precisely observed the vocabulary of the surrounding buildings, such as lighthouses, barns, farmhouses, and shipyards, as well as the shapes and construction of boats. His thorough analysis of these typologies is taken into account when designing in his practice, always skillfully blending the building into the environment. The result is an architecture that is bound to the landscape in the best sense of the vernacular.

As a teacher MacKay-Lyons concerns himself with communicating this approach to his students. He sensitizes them to the historical and cultural roots of Nova Scotia and to the various sites he has chosen for his experiments. He then attempts to awaken local craftsmanship and structural potential in equal measure. In a particularly distinct and interesting scenic location, approximately a hundred kilometers south of Halifax, he initiated an experiment of this kind with the architecture students of Dalhousie University. Over several stages—three of which were realized at the time of my visit—widely varying experiences were brought together.

The design theme of Ghost 3 again related to the themes of landscape, constructional methods, and the sociological context. An elongated, tubelike form twelve feet wide, eight feet high, and one hundred and twenty feet long was erected on undulating ground, hovering over the remains of old walls and striking a new note in the surroundings. The design of the "wind tunnel," as it was called, imparted to architectural students an understanding of the wind forces and the effects they can have on an ultra-lightweight timber structure. (Transverse wind loads can be borne within the timber construction by creating tension-resistant connections.)

Ghost 3 was erected on an existing deck left over from the Ghost 2 project. The structure of Ghost 3 consisted of a series of rigid frame elements, with wind bracing in the longitudinal direction. Recycled construction timber was used for the project. Slender metal strips were inserted for wind bracing, and the outer-wall skin was composed of alternating translucent and transparent panels of corrugated polycarbonate. Open bays allowed glimpses into the interior of the tunnel as well as views out to the surroundings.

The strict form of the structure allowed a precise investigation of different layout possibilities. Rising from the ground, the deck was reminiscent of the indigenous Australian belief, emphasized time and again by Glenn Murcutt, of "touching the earth lightly." The potential for views through the building and out to external vistas set up a dialogue between the building

Ghost 3

Site

and the landscape. Crouched in the landscape, Ghost 3 was the first project in the Ghost Lab to be concerned with recycling materials used in previous projects.

Further steps in this architecture parlante were planned. The story so successfully begun called for a continuation. At the time one could only wish for further stages of this playfully executed and carefully thought-out teaching experiment to continue. Indeed, these were later impressively realized.

The community concert at Ghost 3 also served to commemorate the life and passing of one of the village matriarchs, Beulah Oxner. Photos of her life were projected on the walls of the structure as a background to the concluding celebration with friends and neighbors. The nourishing fish soup, too, which after the site meeting helped to drive away potential evil spirits, will remain in memory forever.

Postscript
The Ghost experiment was not continued until 2002, when it was revived with even greater success in the form of an international summer workshop, with a variety of guests from different architectural practices and schools of architecture. A photo of Ghost 3, reproduced in *Plain Modern* (Princeton Architectural Press, 2005), led me to question how the project had come to what seemed to be a quite dramatic end. Through the course of time, the connections between the posts and the deck rotted. The salty maritime atmosphere did the rest. One day a mighty storm finally brought about the collapse of the tube. Distorted by the powers of nature, the structure continued to pay tribute to its builders in the form of a deconstructivist torso until it was finally dismantled and removed. Once again, nature undeniably had the upper hand over human endeavor.

Ghost 3

Stick-frame silhouette

Translucent roof

Beulah at eighty years old

Ghost 3

Wind tube intersects ruins

Rigid frame

Connection, rigid and braced framing

Ghost 3

Nature wins

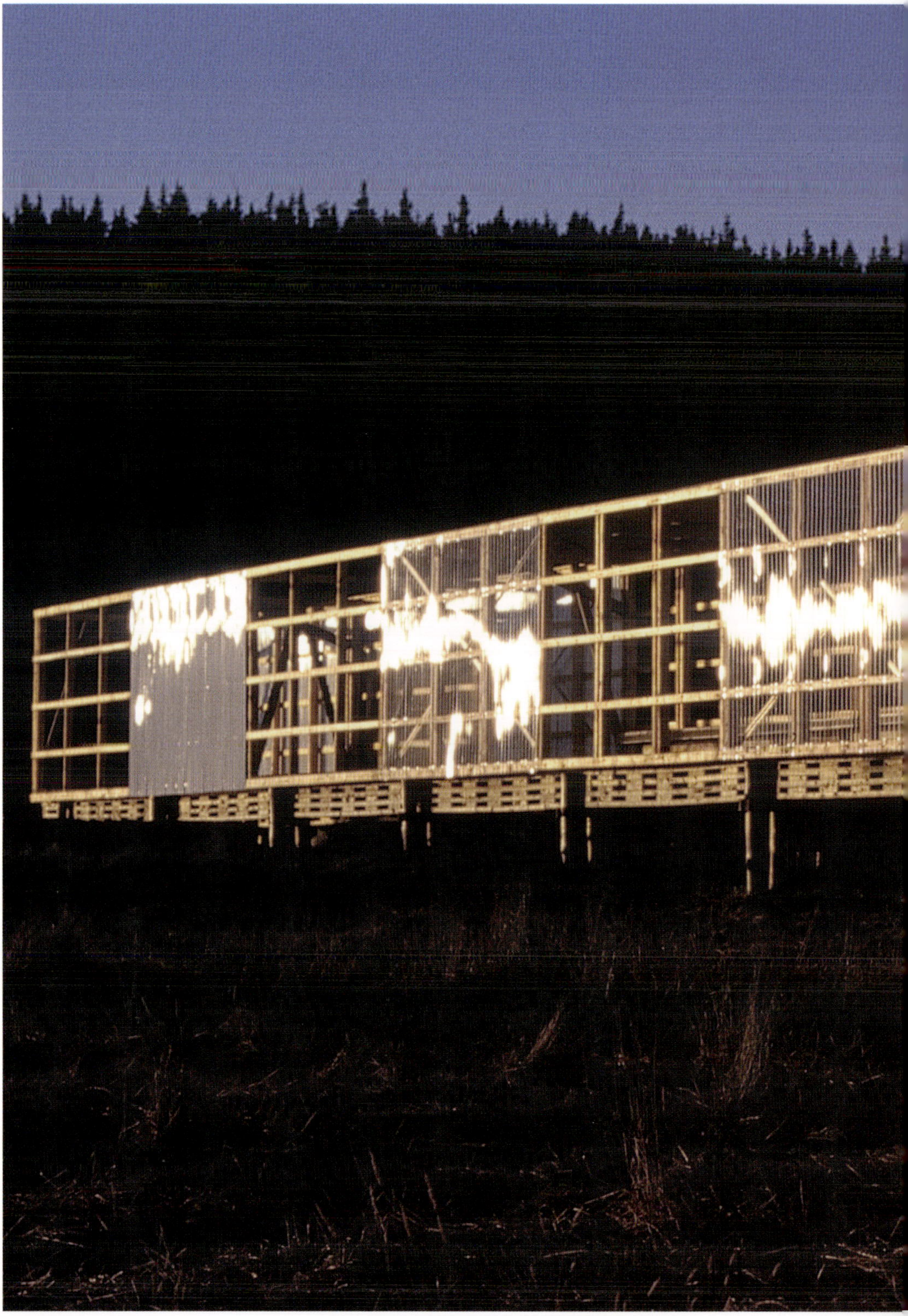

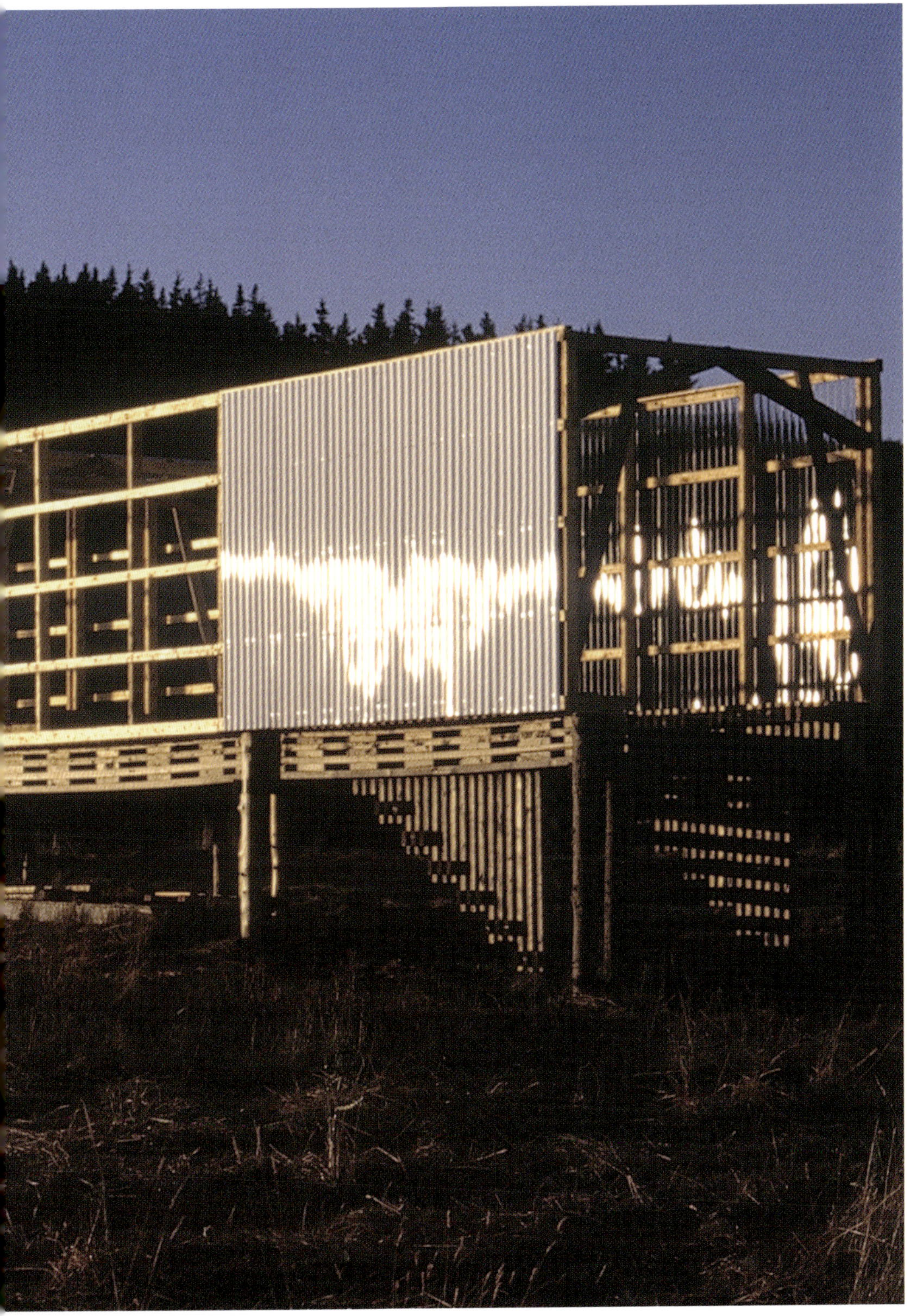

Existe Mande d'Entremont, Brian MacKay-Lyons's grandfather, and his crew

Pots and Pans

Any people will produce a beautiful homogeneous aesthetic if you leave them stagnant long enough. Even their pots and pans will fit their cottages. And if they have had very few pots and pans and haven't invented a new one for five hundred years you can be sure everything fits. In our society nothing fits anything else. Aesthetically every society that changes is thoroughly unsatisfactory.
—Margaret Mead

This was a village at the edge of the world where the life cycle started and ended in a cot in the "borning room," a small room on the ground floor behind the kitchen stove where mothers gave birth. It was also the place where, when they were unable to take the stairs, elders lived until they passed on. In the years between birth and death, the rhythms of life were played out against the patterns of the land, the sea, the seasons. Here, *economy* and *ecology* found their common root meaning (*oikos*, Greek for "house"). Life was a closed loop based on the geomorphology of the place.

Lunenburg County is the drainage basin of the LaHave River. Upriver among its fanning freshwater tributaries were farmers, who engaged in forestry in the winter. They harvested oaks and white pines from the Acadian forest and hauled the logs out with oxen. They floated them downriver, to the tidal portion, to the many shipyards that produced wooden ships to be launched on the tide for the offshore fishery. Teenage boys from this ghost village and other rural villages went off to nearby towns to crew on the schooners that fished the Grand Banks. In the North Atlantic for seasonal trips of three-to-five months, they fished by handline each day for codfish, bobbing up and down in tiny ochre-colored dories. This was dangerous work, not prudent for a married man with a family.

On marrying, a young man returned from the sea to his family home in the village to take up farming, shore fishing, and forestry. The farming was done from late afternoon until dark. In addition to the twelve white houses and the twelve red barns in the village, there were twelve pig houses, twelve chicken houses, four smoke houses, and an assortment of lesser outbuildings. Every family had four oxen—an old team and a young team—and in every team one ox was typically called "lion," and the other "bright." When an ox was too old to work on the farm—pulling logs, carts, and ploughs—it was slow-cooked for a family dinner.

The shore fishing was done on the early morning tide until midafternoon in a double-ender sailing boat. The catch varied by season—groundfish (spring), herring (summer), mackerel (fall), lobsters (winter). Herring was pickled to make Solomon Gundy; cod preserved by salting on drying racks called flakes and used to make a dish called house-banking; cod livers used to make cod-liver oil. Sea-manure was harvested from the beach after the spring storms and hauled with oxcarts onto the land to sweeten the soil in the fields. Fish guts and shellfish were ploughed into the gardens.

The land offered grain, which was ground for bread. Pork and beef were used to make sausage and Lunenburg pudding in sheep's intestines. Wool was used to make clothes and carpets. Many of the fruits of this subsistence agrarian culture were used to provision the Grand Banks schooners during their long voyages. The boy who helped his mom and dad with the haymaking in the summer after classes in the red, one-room schoolhouse became the teenager who went out to sea and later the man who supplied those same ships with materials.

The forestry took place in winter when the sap was out of the trees. Softwoods like spruce, pine, fir, hemlock were harvested for lumber and then milled communally by three-household clusters with a pitsaw. Hardwoods like red oak, white oak, maple, white birch, yellow birch, alder were used to make tools—such as hay rakes, red oxcarts, cart wheels, clothes poles—and for firewood. On the topic of firewood, my friend Max likes to say, "Raond gut mowah last onto'er, ain't it?" (Round wood burns longer than split wood.)

As the story goes, the village had four extended families: Moshers, Romkeys (Oxners), Mossmans, and Hirtles. Each family had three sons and, so, three houses. Each of the twelve houses had a fish-lot property on the back shore, so called because it was back over the hill from the village, next to the site of the Ghost Lab. They shared the net yard, the winch house, and the labor to maintain the breakwater. Every family had a barn of the same oxblood red, with a central threshing floor, an ox stable on one side, and a cattle stable on the other.

Each house was multigenerational, elders were respected, and there were no senior-citizen homes. Each white clapboard house was a cape house (Cape Cod style) with a massive central stone hearth and could be dated by its construction methods.

The earliest were of coulisse construction, a medieval Swiss form of *piece-sur-piece*, a type of building in which a wall of stacked logs is held in place by slotted corner posts, chinked with seaweed, and covered with birchbark building paper. Subsequently, built houses had hewn post-and-beam frames, double-boarded with giant vertical planks. More recent houses were of light stud construction with horizontal sheathing. All of these little, classical houses faced south—regardless of the topography—to catch the most sunlight. A red wooden ladder leaned against the north face of each roof for extinguishing chimney fires. Every kitchen had a Lunenburg Foundry wood-burning cookstove surrounded by four Boston rockers made from their own wood lot, each on its own braided rag rug. Like snowflakes they were all different but all the same: maple for the curved rockers, birch for the rungs, and soft pine for the seat.

Then there was the land. The settlers did not have a primogeniture system for land inheritance. Rather, it was subdivided among all of the children on a democratic basis. As a result, each household owned a hilltop grain piece, mowlands for hay, a piece of swampland for ox-pasture between the hills, berry-picking grounds, woodlots, and a home piece. Each home piece contained all of the buildings—houses, barns, and sheds—an orchard, vegetable garden, a rhubarb patch, a flower patch, and cordwood piles. The home pieces were clustered together in the village in the extended-family pattern, with a single shared barnyard. The twelve households in the village shared ownership of the commons (woodlands) and the manure yard (place for leeching salt from sea-manure).

This material culture was sustained for hundreds of years. When agriculture thrived, forests were burned off to the sea to create more farmland; when agriculture failed, forest overtook the fields again. This cycle has been broken. The world's best fishing grounds have been depleted, the native forests have regrown with genetically inferior species. The small, hilly subsistence farms worked by oxen have been supplanted by fewer, larger farms worked with machinery. Once everyone was a farmer; now there are few.

The site of Ghost Lab is the site of the abandoned ghost village. The barns, the houses, the fish sheds—they are all gone. In the 1940s, the young men went off to war. After they had seen the world, they were less interested in returning home to marry their cousins. Today, this site contains the ruins of some thirty former "permanent" structures. In the spring one can see the rhubarb and the daffodils come up, describing the daily lives of those who went before. If you close your eyes, you can almost smell the laundry on the clotheslines in the salt air.

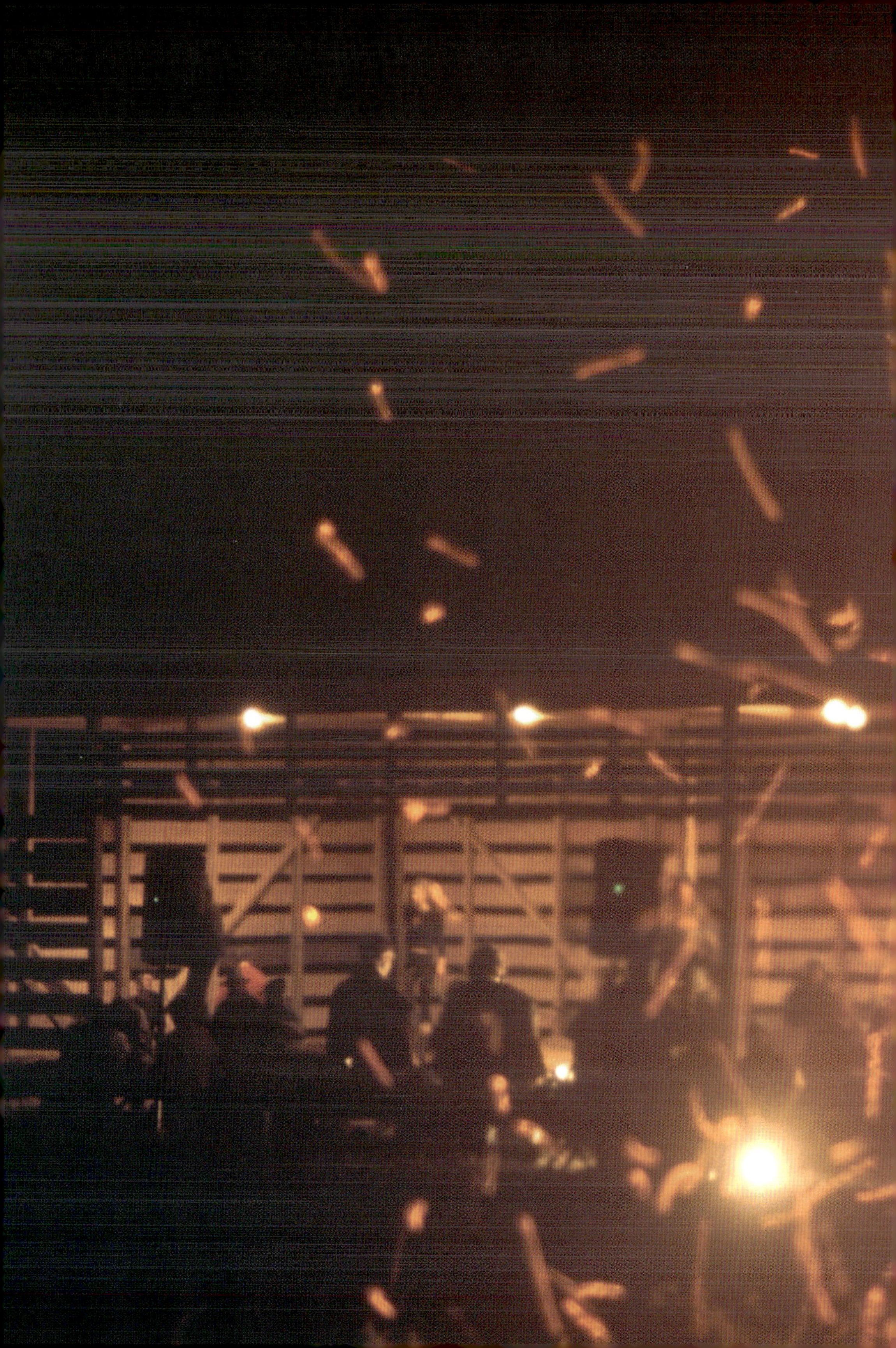

GHOST 4

June 29 to July 14, 2002

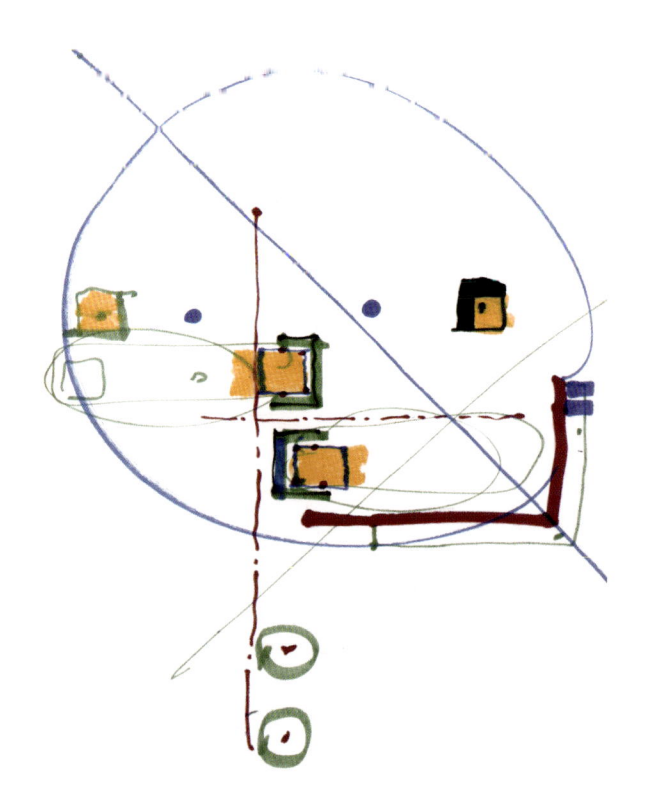

The Bones of Ghosts: Structuring the Ephemeral

Robert Ivy

From a promontory high above the sea in Nova Scotia, Brian MacKay-Lyons backs up his assertions about the nature of architecture, working and teaching at one metaphorical end of the earth. The vantage point from his farm, which overlooks the Atlantic Ocean, offers a unique perspective, allowing the architect to consider the tensions inherent in a coastline, in the meaning of human intervention in such a prodigious natural environment, and in the balance between abstraction of art and architecture with the demands of the real world. When he chose to live and practice there, returning to the province of his birth, the farm he found south of Halifax, Canada, seemed the perfect spot to build and to share his ideas with students.

MacKay-Lyons has strong ideas about the state of teaching: too much has run to words and to the abstract, when architecture essentially deals with building. Too often, schools have omitted real-world questions, such as architecture's social and economic components. His experience as a teacher at Dalhousie University in Halifax has included involvement with free labs and cooperative education. His goal in establishing the Ghost Lab was to merge the two.

By founding a residential program and inviting students from Canada, the United States, and internationally to Nova Scotia, he hoped to "reconfirm the idea of the architect/master builder tradition," relying on the apprenticeship method of teaching in a real place. In the process of introducing students to design-build, he interjected a key element, "directed play," which augmented the more pragmatic goals. Much like the director of a film, MacKay-Lyons gives the actors (students/architects) a frame of mind to work in and then lets them create a masterpiece.

While the program could be located virtually anywhere, the remote location, near the site of the earliest continental settlements by Europeans and where the next landfall across the ocean is Portugal, offers a unique setting for learning. According to the architect, it is a place that is both grounded in geography, soil, wind, water, and history yet "capable of abstraction." This tension fuels the work of his practice and inspires the projects that each class encounters.

For the fourth occasion, MacKay-Lyons's students gathered on a spot drenched in Canadian and North American history. Within a quarter-mile of his own house lie the bones—the remnants, foundations, stones, and artifacts—of early Acadian and German settlements. Samuel de Champlain's expeditionary force made its first landfall in the New World there at the mouth of the LaHave River in 1604. This site for the Ghost projects was originally farmed by families whose descendents still live in the area—purchased by the architect nearly four centuries later—and underlies each construction project.

The architect/teacher enriches and speeds the acquisition of knowledge, having spent a lifetime studying the deep background of the place. He transmits knowledge of village elders, including how to construct a way of life connected to the weather and land. MacKay-Lyons reaches back to geologic time in describing the land, how the ice age sculpted the hillsides into a series of diagonal moraines and set the pattern for human settlement.

The terrain and weather shaped the first buildings, which inform the decisions about new buildings. From his farm, "within walking distance," he has, in his practice, constructed simple forms drawn from the vernacular yet clarified and transformed into modern thought. The Ghost Lab follows similar principles. Three inspirations underlie the program and animate most decisions: The first is the land and the landscape, which "slows you to the beginnings" of architecture. The second is the actual community of inhabitants that surround his farm. And third, the program draws its roots from the material culture already present—how have people built before; what can be learned from them? Culture in all its forms—high- to lowbrow—shapes the construction projects.

As a former student of the late Charles Moore, MacKay-Lyons admits that he is "part control-freak, part participatory designer." The students are organized honestly, with leaders and teachers and learners. "The program is not about self-discovery, [a way to] terrorize people." Instead, he harks back to time-honored traditions, including the guild system, which provides a clear route for others to follow. At the same time, the student group derives strength from teamwork, "a pedagogical goal," avoiding solo performances to achieve productivity through group effort in a short time. The construction crew, made up of architects-to-be, takes on the tasks of measuring and sawing and carting and climbing and hammering under the direction of an experienced contractor, who doles out the tasks based on ability and experience.

Yet how to inspire them to action? In 2002, the genesis of the Ghost Lab lay in one question: "What would it feel like to stand between two barns that once stood there?" Sited on the historic peninsula at the mouth of the LaHave River, the Ghost Lab tells a story through architecture, employing early settlement patterns that point to alternative ways of organizing the world. His method materializes the space between the barns of two brothers—"kissing cousins," he calls the demolished barns. That spot, as wide as a tractor road, became the power

Ghost 4

Chainsaw model

Student making model

Study model

Ghost 4

Noah's Ark

Sorting

Grounding

Ghost 4

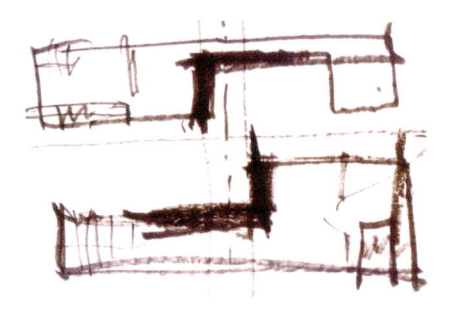

Two facades

point between two farms, the abstract expression of human settlement, which MacKay-Lyons transforms into simple structure.

As wind and weather shaped early structures, each Ghost Lab structure is shaped by elementary constraints. In Ghost 4, a limited budget dictated wood members—a renewable material—simply joined. Where the two ancient barns had sat, budget and materials suggested a single structure, which extruded into a singular gateway to the sea, its members alternated and interlocked, stretched apart like the fingers of a hand.

Transformational, responsive thinking was required. The team identified that the original foundation stones demanded a rational bay spacing, suggesting that the Ghost structure comprise four bays rather than the traditional three. In the masterbuilder tradition, the team took a "come/see" attitude, doubling the exterior siding of the pavilion while under construction to enhance the apparent solidity of the object from afar: you had to see it to understand it in three dimensions.

On the final day in mid-July, participants stopped all work to celebrate the work of their own hands. A community of locals, including neighbors and musicians and friends, trooped down the hillside to find the Ghost pavilion glowing on the headland, illuminated by electric lights and a bonfire glowing in the ruined foundations of the original farmhouse. An Acadian singer and a bagpiper overlaid the evening with sound, as the group stood buffeted by the wind.

MacKay-Lyons will continue to design and to build there as long as his neighbors show up for the party. "I could spend the rest of my life building on the site, and there is almost nothing there." Nothing but soil and history, people and communities and ideas that have gone before, and the memories of four contemporary projects that have celebrated and transformed this matrix into architecture. Still, the students come.

Ghost 4

Modulation

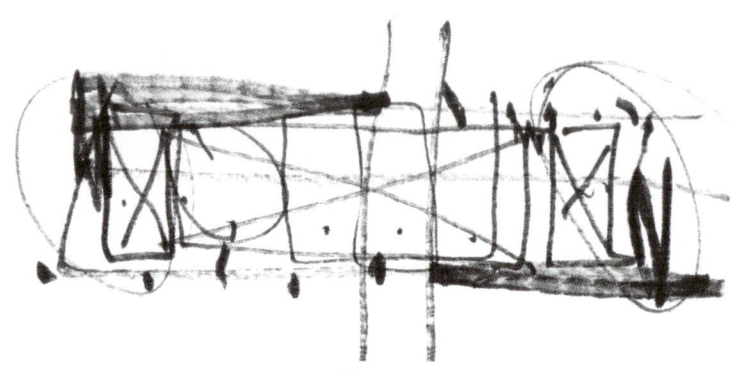

Schema

Ghost 4

Consummation

Lobster feast

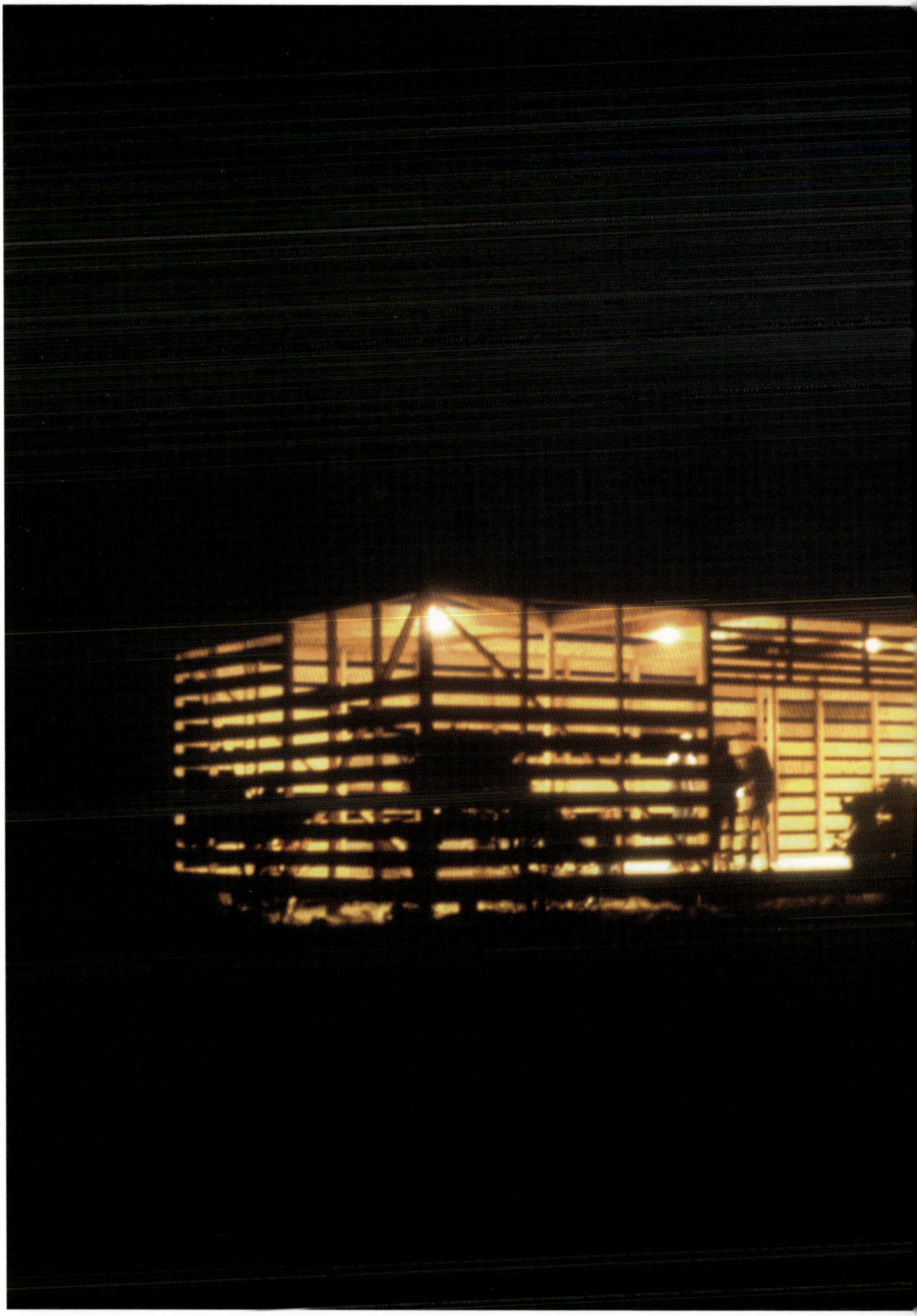

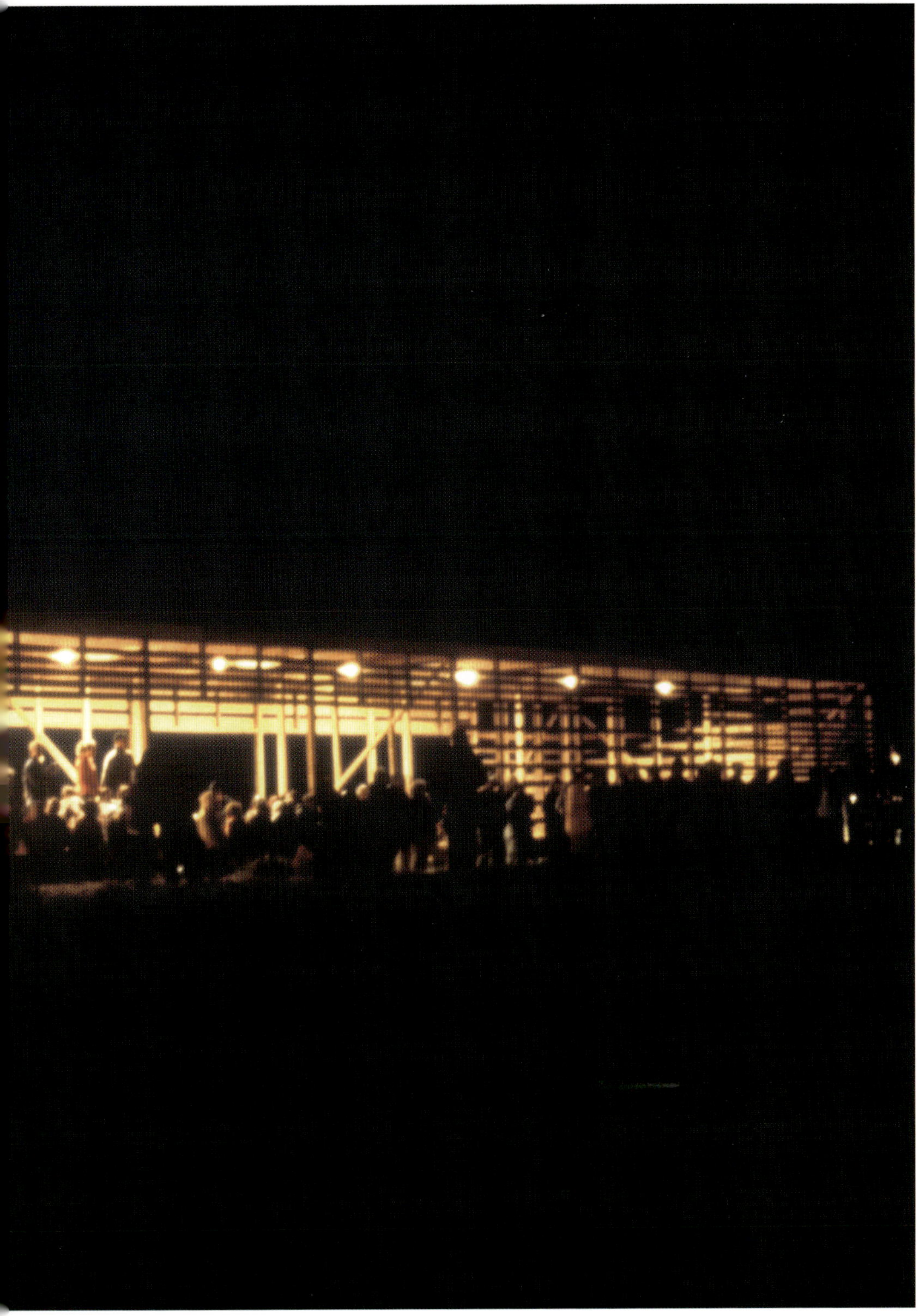

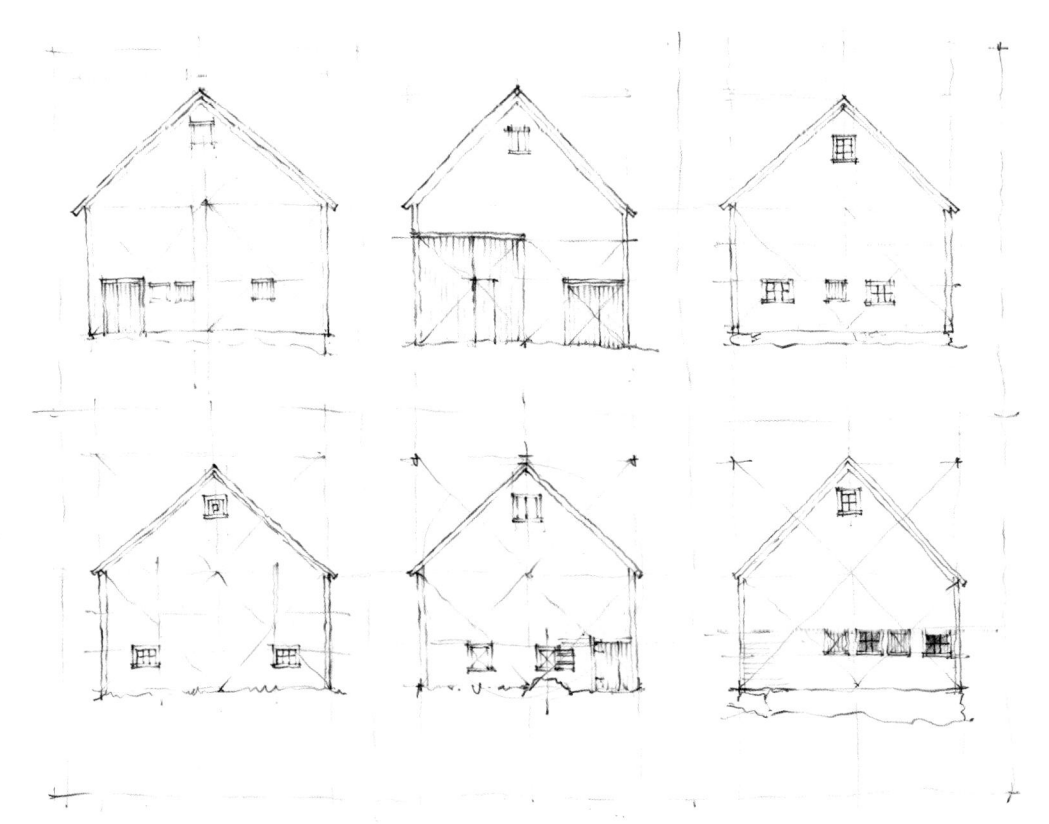

Barn studies

Why Albert Oxner Shingled His Barn

Brian, come down and sit a piece, and we'll yarn a spell.
—Albert Oxner

My neighbor Albert Oxner could neither read nor write, yet he possessed a deeply cultivated intelligence about both nature and culture. One evening, not long before the village elder died, he told me the story of why he and his father decided to shingle his barn.

> One morning when I was young, my dad and I decided to change the barn around. It used to be double-boarded up and down between the heavy timbers, but it got rotten from the weather. We stripped off the double-boarding, and we put studs in between the old timbers. Then we covered them with horizontal boards across. On this we put shingles. We took the oil from the livers of the cod we caught and mixed it up with iron-oxide powder and ox blood. This we would paint onto the shingles. If you put a drop on a shingle one night, by the next day it would soak right through to the other side. It had a "good" smell, but it was some stuff to make the shingles last.

In vernacular architecture, advances in building practices usually take place gradually. This organic process is often lost when, with a historian's perspective, a building is categorized as post-and-beam or stick-frame construction after the fact. The story of Albert and his dad's renovation pinpoints the critical shift in construction thinking from a heavy-timber system that was brought from Europe, to a light-timber one that emerged in North America over the last 250 years. This technological revolution resulted in the disarmingly simple platform-frame construction that dominates North American domestic building today.

Architectural technology historian Tom Peters discusses the distinction between Old World and New World attitudes toward technology in his 1989 article "An American Culture of Construction" in *Perspecta 25: The Yale Architecture Journal.* He explains how the genius of light-timber framing is a response to the conditions of vast geography, a shortage of skilled labor, shrinking lumber dimensions, and, most importantly, the advent of the cheap, soon-to-become-common nail connector. The proliferation of the use of many economical connections achieves great structural plasticity by dispersing wind loads in a structure through multiple load paths. The result is an unexpectedly stronger and more supple structure. Man-made design, in this case, simulates design in nature. This structural redundancy is analogous to neuroplasticity in the human brain.

In North America, pragmatism is an elevated cultural virtue that Europeans have difficulty appreciating. The ultimate strength that comes from a democratic, nonhierarchical light-timber-frame tradition has taken on political meaning in the New World. North American architects have become somewhat marginalized within the building industry, designing only a small percentage of buildings. Their wood designs typically favor elemental, heavy-timber structures while the construction industry employs the more economic, environmentally sustainable, structurally superior light-timber frame.

In Nova Scotia, there is a longstanding relationship with stick-building. The building carpenters were the ships' carpenters. Young boys would build ships on the beach in summer with their fathers and buildings in the winter. The large Grand Banks schooners and the square-rigged clipper ships utilized heavy-sawn rib framing. The shore fishery, however, developed a light-timber frame that is analogous to contemporary, domestic-platform framing. The ubiquitous Cape Island boat used in the lobster fishery is the ultimate light-timber "basket." (The half-inch-thick steamed ribs are only three inches apart.) These resilient workhorses of the shore fishery can break half of their ribs pounding against the rocks and still limp home for supper without sinking.

The Ghost Lab projects, and houses designed by MacKay-Lyons Sweetapple Architects, are conceived as torsion boxes, which transfer wind forces through their monolithic skins like the Cape Islander. The elemental expression of roofs and walls gives way to the idea of the skin as a continuous wrapper. Overhanging eaves often disappear completely. As the free plan has been fundamental to the modern architecture movement, the idea of the "free skin" is central to the work of MacKay-Lyons Sweetapple Architects. The firm delights in the relative freedom in composing building fenestration; the awareness that one can whack holes just about anywhere in stick-built skins without compromising their structural integrity. In order to demonstrate this design freedom, openings are often placed in painfully awkward relationships to one another or large portions of the envelope are removed altogether. These tactics result in chameleon-like structures that are at once both monumentally pure, solid forms and dangerously flimsy-looking shrink-wraps.

The extremely changeable maritime climate, with its frequent freeze/thaw, wet/dry cycles, is a real taskmaster. It also favors a monolithic building skin of a single material, thereby avoiding differential coefficients of expansion. Wood is a very adaptable and forgiving material. The wood-shingled skins of the buildings are constantly moving and out of focus—their four layers of shingles are like the feathers of a duck, keeping it dry in the water. Ironically, in this climate, overhangs can cause leaks by creating ice dams over cold eaves with snow melting behind them due to heated interiors below. This aversion to overhangs, based on building performance, contributes to the monolithic, zero aesthetic of the designs.

Albert's barn, like most of the barns of Lunenburg County, were renovated constantly. When house windows were replaced, the old windows were often reused in the barns. Additions employed the most current framing practices and, therefore, varied from the host barn. Rotting windward and seaward faces of barns were often replaced. Old barns were cannibalized or mined for replacement material; some were burned for the nails, at a time before blacksmiths were plentiful. This wood-based material-culture tradition fosters an organic view of history. The prototypical Lunenburg barn is a variation on the English barn type, with a central, double-height threshing floor, flanked on either side by stables for oxen and cattle, and with haylofts above. This recurring form is a familiar icon in the landscape. Although no two English barns are identical, they are all fundamentally the same. Like old friends such as Albert, many of these have disappeared.

From listening and watching my elders, I have become progressively more interested in a process-oriented view of culture. The Australian Pritzker Laureate architect Glenn Murcutt asserts the most interesting architectural question: "How did this building get here?" One day I watched three ships' carpenters at Snyder's Shipyard, upriver from the Ghost Lab site, saw a huge ship rib out of a block of oak. One guy turned a wheel that tilted the table-saw platter from side to side. Another turned a wheel that tilted the platter forward and backward. The third guided the oak block through the saw blade, following a single sensuous pencil line. They worked in unison without a word about what they were doing. Instead, they chattered only about the previous evening's hockey game. Like Albert, they may not have known how to read or write, but material culture was embodied in them.

This cultural power is lost on most contemporary architects. It is dangerous for our profession to become detached from culture and society. Cultural intelligence is the result of thousands of people thinking and acting over hundreds of years. No individual can match this alone. Glenn Murcutt describes his own buildings as "semi-tailored garments": 80 percent designed by culture, 20 percent by him.

As for Albert and his dad, that summer morning that they shingled the barn, they were just trying to be modern—to utilize the latest technology. They were engaged in the pragmatic search for better building practices that responded to their environment, its available materials, and the particular climate.

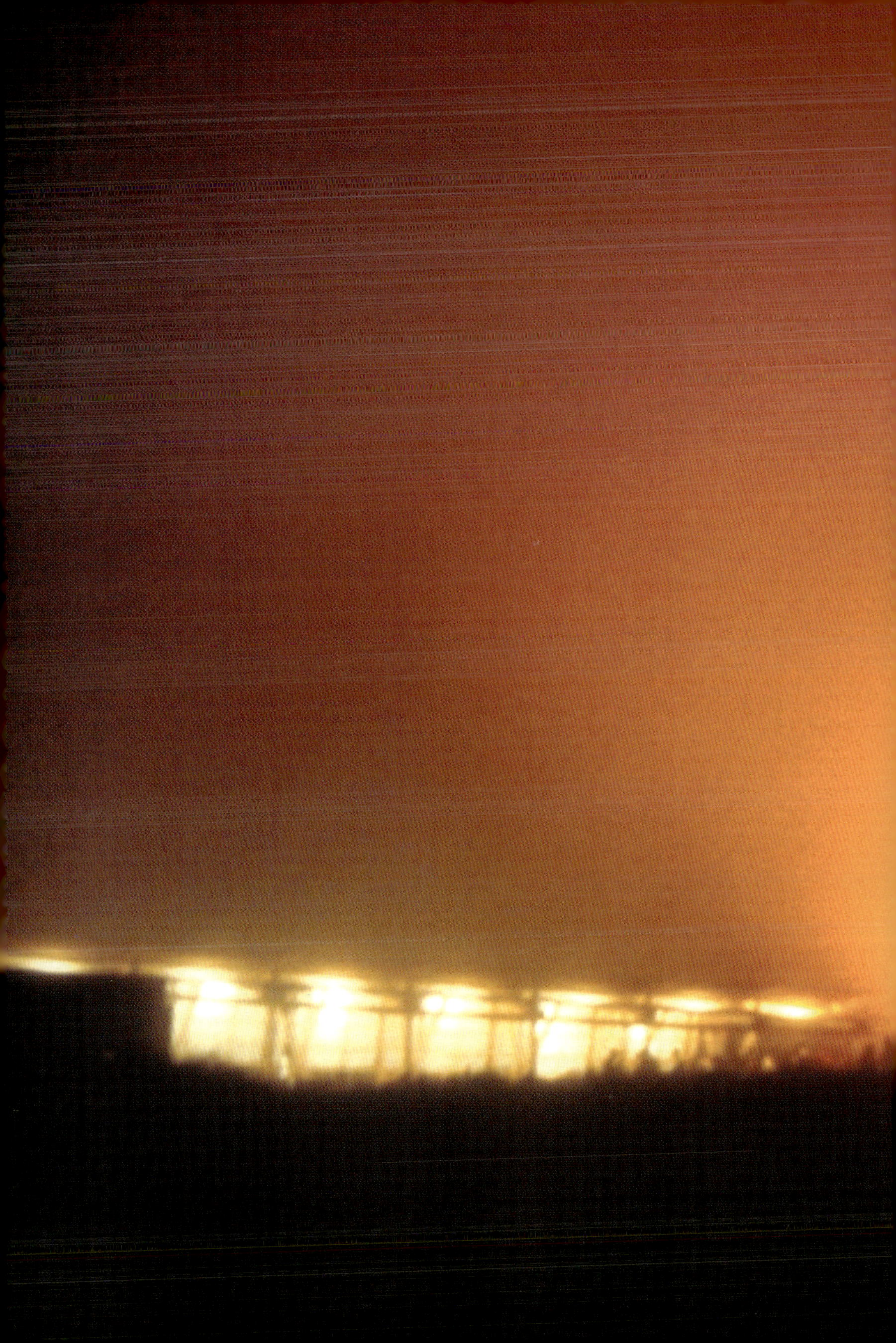

GHOST 5

June 28 to July 13, 2003

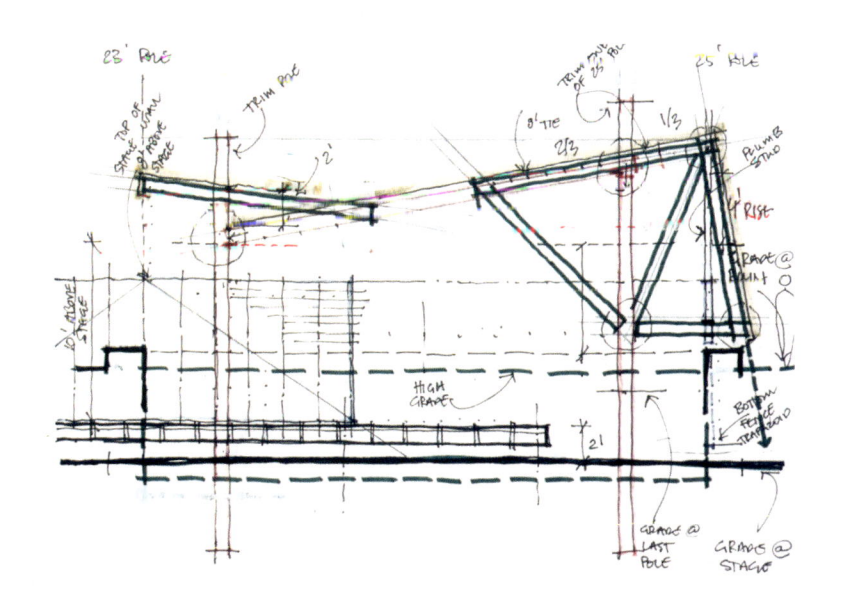

On the Fringes of the Empire

Kenneth Frampton

Brian MacKay-Lyons's annual summer school, known by the sobriquet Ghost, is what he calls "a crash course in material culture." Until now, this spirit under discussion has taken the form of a temporary timber structure built largely with student labor, aided and abetted by the assistance of local experts including, on this occasion, the builder Gordon MacLean, the engineer Michel Comeau, and MacKay-Lyons himself. In this regard it could be seen as a gesture arising out of the region itself—the partially conscious product of an unreal summerland of rolling grassland, unexpected lakes, and endless stands of spruce set before the sea. Since it can hardly be seen as a summer school in the usual sense, it is perhaps more appropriate to think of it as a hands-on experience or even as a guerilla course in large-scale carpentry. It was, in any event, no easy ride as I was to witness firsthand on the occasion of the topping-out ceremony that brought this latest Dewey-esque exercise to a dramatic close.

This event was the occasion for a musical evening, complete with a roaring bonfire fed by leftover timber scattered about the foundations of an old stone house. It was, one might say, a setting out of E. Annie Proulx's the *Shipping News* (Scribner, 1993) and with unforeseen fireworks firing off into the night. Sustained by hot toddies and shielded from the penetrating chill by a motley assembly of ground sheets, camp chairs, and sundry blankets, the audience assembled itself before the improvised stage, its elevated rough-hewn boards supporting a further display of local talent, including the Bluenose Fiddlers, the extremely urbane Ian McKinnon—equally adept with flute and bagpipe—and, finally, the guitar and voice of the heroic Lennie Gallant. All of this would be played out against the restless presence of an impenetrable fog permeating the land as it rose from the invisible surface of the sea. Was this perhaps the ultimate ghost, the deeper, older spirit of place brought into being by the music and an audacious structure, shining forth in the night?

    The fifth Ghost structure rested on sixteen columns at twelve-foot centers, arranged in two lines virtually twenty-four feet apart, yielding a seven-bay structure with each bay being a double square. The fact that the land sloped from north to south—that is to say from the stage up to the ruined house—meant that this underlying geometrical order was difficult to discern: the height of the columns ranged from eighteen feet at the northern end to some twelve feet at the southern limit of the structure. The columns comprised pressure-treated wooden telegraph poles, buried some six feet into the ground, depending on the fall of the site. These elements tapered from around eleven inches in diameter at the butt to some eight inches at the crown, an entasis that was barely perceptible over the heights involved. The inclined clear-span beams were also made of telegraph poles, with each composite beam—comprised of two poles—bearing on ledgers. These double beams were scalloped around the columns; the entire assembly was bolted together with 5/8-inch-diameter stainless-steel threaded rods with matching nuts and washers. The knee joints at the apex of the roof were reinforced by two-inch galvanized metal straps. The finished structure assumed the form of an inclined roof running over the frame and hanging down on the ocean side to become a screen. This skeleton was finally covered with muslin, bestowing upon the nocturnal Ghost the character of a luminous wing or lantern.

Ghost 5

Stereotonic and tectonic

Structural parti

Pole barn

Ghost 5

Lantern

Kenneth Frampton, barn lecture

Michel Comeau, Talbot Sweetapple, and Gordon MacLean (construction expert)

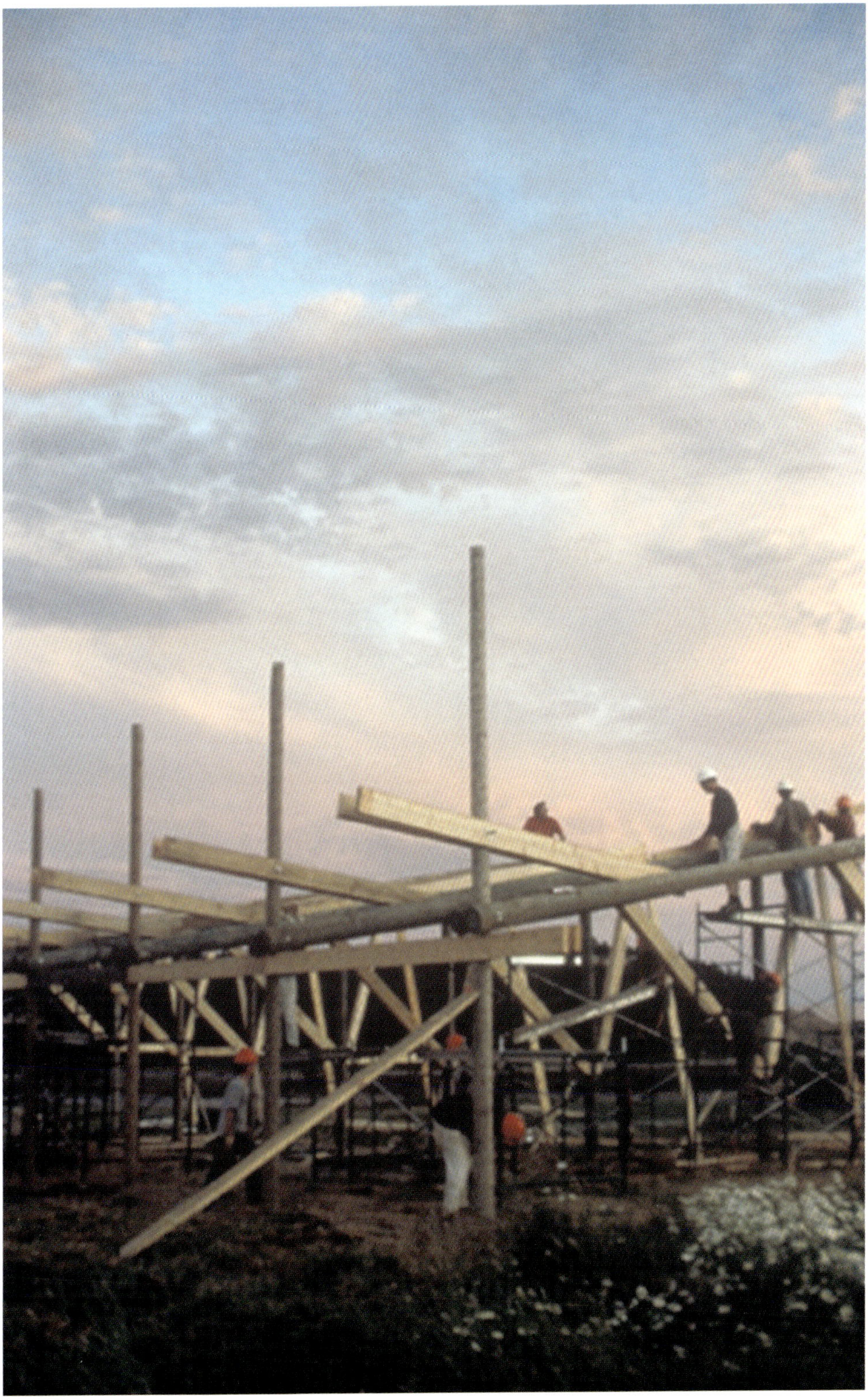

Ghost 5

Floating

Fiddler

Gathering

The point of departure for this improbable structure seems to have been a conceptual sketch by MacKay-Lyons, on the basis of which the students developed and realized the work—the first week spent on evolving the joints and the second on erecting the frame. With the exception of power tools and a backhoe, the whole undertaking was an exercise in pre–machine age ingenuity, a literal barn raising employing a block and tackle for hoisting the roof beams.

What may we now read into the quasi-permanent existence of this structure as it stands alone and unattended before the sea? Perhaps we should think of it as something more than a structure. In fact, it could be said that its ultimate function is to serve as a landscape marker, as a kind of sky-sign. The Ghost projects suggest all sorts of uncharted possibilities for the future of the site, and perhaps this is the ultimate intention behind the gesture: an evocation of the hamlet that once stood on this site before the sea.

One is reminded by all of this of another self-conscious seafront settlement totally isolated by design from the ideological outreach of imperialism. I have in mind the Open City of Ritoque in Chile, dating from the mid 1960s, the utopian sand-dune settlement of Amerida, designed by Alberto Cruz, that sets itself up in self-conscious opposition to the gringo culture of the north. Although we are quite removed from this in Halifax, the difference is not so far as one might at first imagine—for the spirit lying behind this northern Ghost runs wide and deep. There is a cultural undertow here that not so incidentally recalls the lost culture of the Acadians, brutally expelled from these shores in 1755. This is still perhaps then the stuff of which, despite our globalized world, some kind of cultural resistance may yet be enjoined.

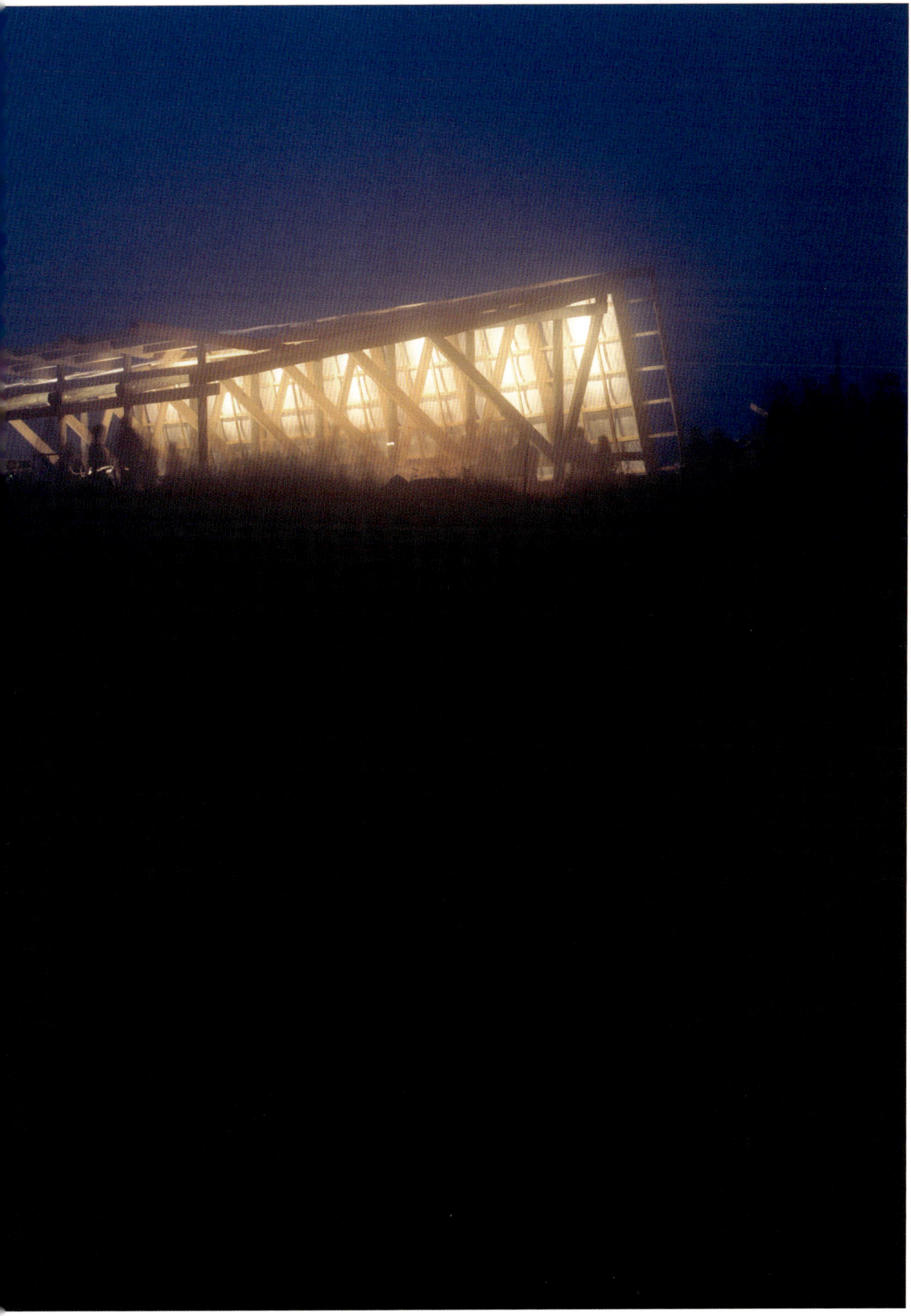

Oxner and oxen

Barnyard

There is no connection between the basilica and the bicycle shed....
The basilica is architecture, the bicycle shed is mere building.
—Nikolas Pevsner

Nova Scotia is a narrow, 375-mile-long landform floating off the Atlantic coast of North America, following the diagonal axis (northeast to southwest) of the Eastern Seaboard. It is the Appalachian Mountain Ridge gone out to sea. This diagonal means that the typical view to the ocean and the solar orientation are typically not quite aligned. As a result, the geometry of things cultural (buildings, roads, hedgerows, stone walls, etc.) in Nova Scotia tends to be orthogonal to this diagonal coastline while the geometry of things natural (sun and wind) follows the cardinal points of the compass. By extension, the building forms of the work of MacKay-Lyons Sweetapple Architects are sited according to the cultural, geometric order while the building skins, with their openings (doors and windows), are pulled around like loose clothing to address the demands of the sun and the wind. We delight in this contradiction.

In Lunenburg County, the glacial hills—drumlins—reinforce this duet between cultural and natural ordering systems.

The drumlins are perpendicular to the coast, on a northwest/southeast axis. Every fertile hill once had a red barn and a white farmhouse whose roof ridgelines followed its long axis. These building forms always pinwheeled with each other to create a south-facing barnyard. This disarmingly primitive, agrarian strategy is a protourban placemaking gesture that forms the basis for great public places and city forms. From Siena's medieval campo to the neighborhood squares of Savannah, Georgia, these public spaces are grown-up versions of the barnyard.

This brings us once again to our ghost village, where twenty-five years ago my wife and I bought a 1750s farmstead with a red barn and white house. Ever since, I have been an amateur anthropologist, studying my own barnyard in order to discover timeless architectural principles that question the fit between nature and culture. Weathering—the effects of the sun and wind—dictates architectural responses. It is the south-facing sides of buildings that suffer most from the freeze/thaw, wet/dry cycles—the north facades have more stable climatic conditions. I have learned that, in this place, 80 percent of the winds come from the west, precipitation from the southwest, and the sparkling, dry, champagne winds from the northwest. And that the occasional spring or fall nor'easter can rip your roof off.

The modest collection of historic buildings in our barnyard and, more importantly, the spaces between them have been the principle source of inspiration for the design work of MacKay-Lyons Sweetapple Architects—in the landscape and in the city, in houses and public buildings, in the village and abroad. For example, the Cape house with its massive central stone hearth is the symbol of family, marking the center of our universe. The English barn with its double-height central threshing floor and flanking stables and haylofts is the prototype for much of the history of public architecture. After all, the erudite architectural historian Nikolas Pevsner must have known that *basilica* is just the Roman word for barn. The minor sheds such as our chicken house or tractor shed, with their thru spaces, participate in the barnyard-making game and invite the landscape to flow through them. There is a Tuscan barn inside every Renaissance cathedral.

There is considerable talk today, both within the architectural discourse and within our broader society, regarding the topic of environmental sustainability. This is fundamentally a good thing. But the modern movement idea of the city as a machine for living, with its infatuation with technology, has caused a kind of cultural amnesia regarding older, more sustainable building practices. Let us avoid a new technocratic priesthood of greenwashing experts. We must remember that environmental sustainability is not just a new fashion, but an ancient practice. Unlike Professor Nikolas Pevsner (who sees no connection between architecture and building), I would urge our discipline to look at the likes of the lowly barnyard. Most vernacular building culture has displayed a kind of pragmatic sustainability. The understanding of a farmer regarding both environmentally and culturally sustainable practices constitutes most of what is important to know—how to create microclimates, how to passively heat and cool both interior and exterior spaces, how to use the winds to ventilate, and how to use locally available, renewable materials and skills. Remember, both economy and ecology share the same root meaning. The vernacular is simply what you do when you can't afford to get it wrong.

For years I have climbed up and over the hill from our 1750s barnyard on clear winters' days with my dog and my chainsaw to clear the land that was to become the site for the Ghost Lab. I looked down on historic ruins, searching to find the organizing principles of a lost settlement. The early Ghost Lab constructions (Ghosts 1 through 5) were temporary structures, employing designing and building as research strategies, palpating the landscape for meaning. Subsequent Ghosts (6 through 9) produced so-called permanent and semipermanent structures. A barnyard fence now formalizes the line between the permanent cottages and studio inside the compound and the semipermanent tower and barn just outside the fence. Permanent structures have concrete foundations while semipermanent structures have pole foundations. These new structures occur among, but not on top of, the old ruins—they speak to and listen to the ruins. Like my neighbor Albert Oxner, the ruins say, "Brian, come down and sit a piece, and we'll yarn a spell."

It is not surprising that this newly constituted barnyard, produced by the Ghost Lab projects among the ruins, displays many of the qualities of the 1750s barnyard over the hill. Like the historic barnyard, it is the charged places between, even more than the object quality of the buildings, that is important—the protected body-scaled places, the comfortable outdoor microclimates, the choreographic effect of constantly changing perspectives moving through this landscape. All of these contribute to a sense of place in the environment. An idealized, protourban court, formed by the pinwheeling relationship between cottages and studio, emerges and implies a diagonal south axis. All of the skins of these buildings are oriented south so that their glazing faces south to maximize solar gain. There are now two courtyards—one is a grassy ceremonial square where Ghost concerts are held, the other is a working barnyard for horses, cattle, and tractors. The simple game of pinwheeling barnyards can continue to fold out in this valley floor at the edge of the sea for years to come. Some new structures will be added while others are erased and recycled for their materials.

Today, sitting in the new studio (Ghost 8) writing this essay, I am looking out at a foggy barnyard. The fog gives the barnyard a more interior feeling, allowing me to imagine that it is some great urban space.

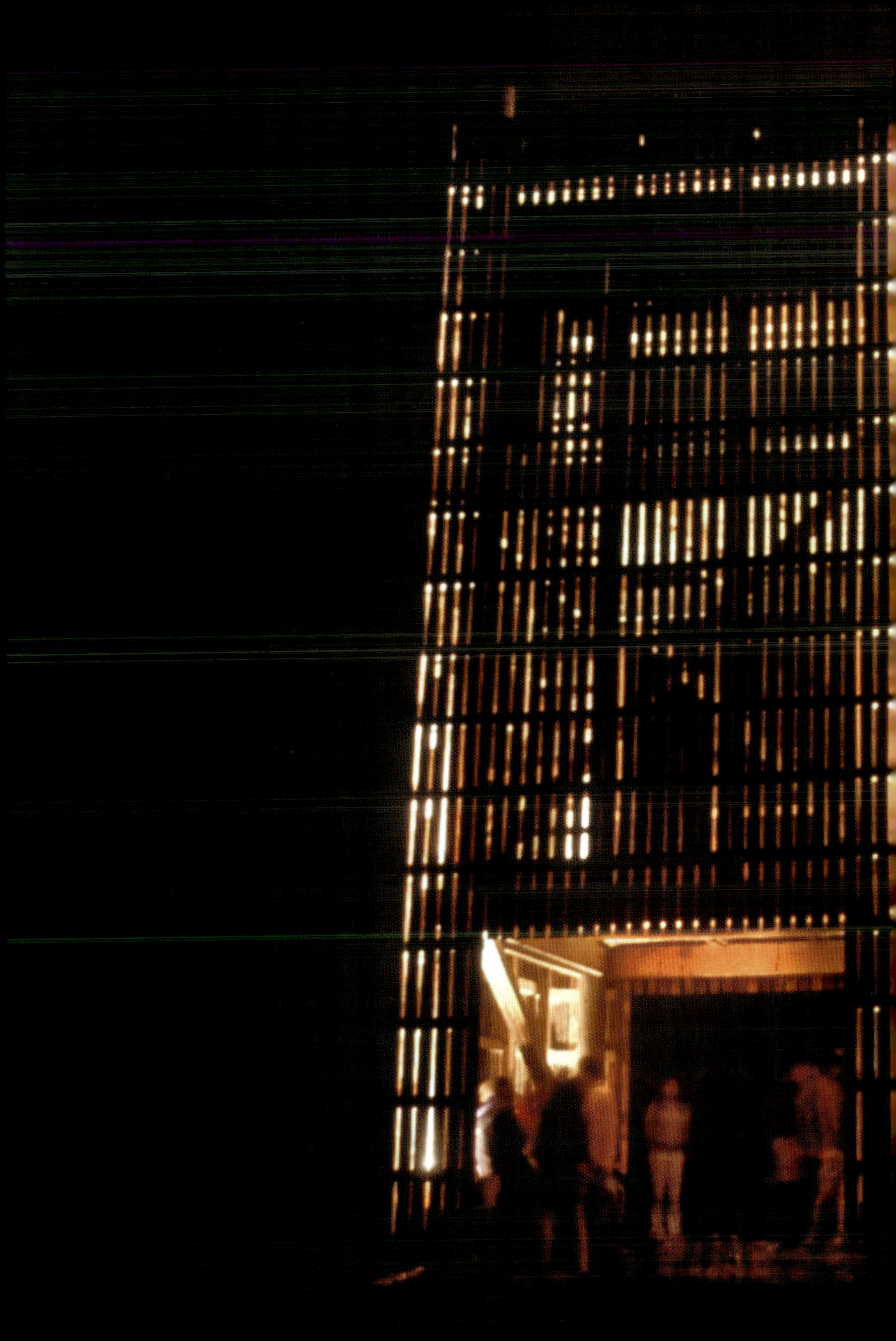

GHOST 6

July 3 to July 18, 2004

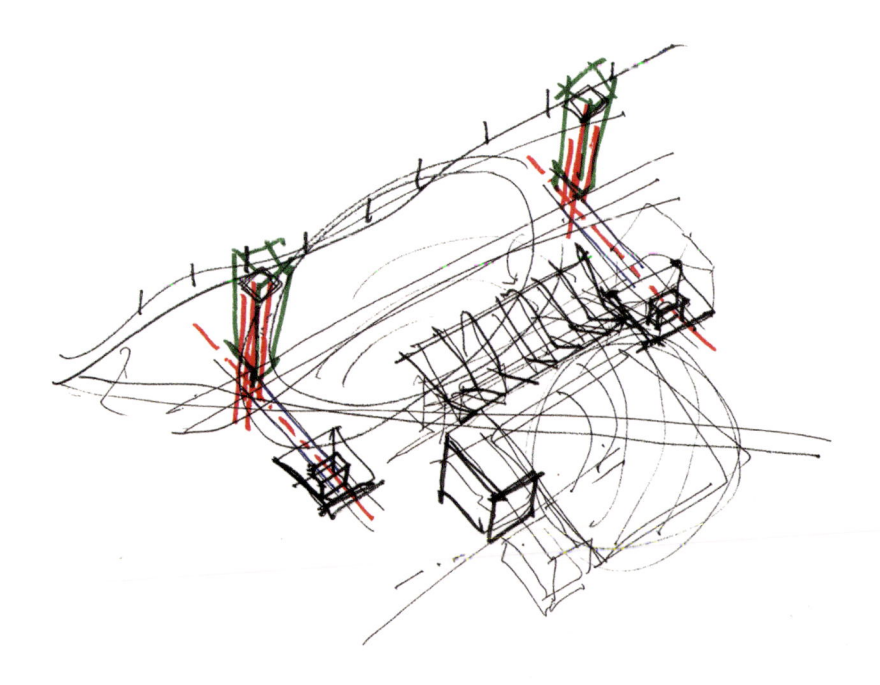

Seeing Ghosts

Thomas Fisher

You can go to Nova Scotia to see ghosts. The Ghost project site has a haunted quality. The ocean-estuary location stands near where the French first landed on the North American continent in 1604, beginning that culture's long and tumultuous history on these shores. What would North America be like had the French penchant for trading and coexisting with the aboriginal people dominated over the English desire for land and conquest? What would have happened to our natural environment had immigrating Europeans adopted the ways of the native cultures, rather than impose foreign patterns of settlement?

  The Ghost projects offer one possible answer. Built almost entirely of local lumber, the structures recalled the biodegradable buildings that the French fur traders erected during their early settlement in North America. Constructing their trading posts entirely of local timber, the French would burn down the buildings when no longer needed, culling iron nails and other fasteners from the ashes for reuse in the next structure. With one exception, MacKay-Lyons has had the past Ghost projects dismantled and their parts reused in subsequent years, a lesson in how we might all start to build with the goal of leaving little or no trace behind.

  Also haunting the projects' site are the ruins of the three farmsteads and a fishing port that once stood there. Owned by brothers Simeon and Wilson Mosher, the farmsteads' former houses and barns now exist as stone-lined depressions in the ground, like open graves that speak to the hard lives spent living off that land. Never an easy place to farm, Nova Scotia still has an intact fishing economy, whose material culture MacKay-Lyons draws from in his architecture. Indeed, the incredible power of his work comes, in part, from the powerfully moving quality of that vernacular culture. The Moshers, like many farming families, gave up the ghost around World War II and abandoned their property for easier lives elsewhere.

    A new wave of immigrants has begun to occupy the land: wealthier urban dwellers have started to resettle rural Nova Scotia, buying up the old farmsteads for second homes and retirement retreats. That includes MacKay-Lyons himself, who owns part of the old Mosher farm on which the Ghost projects have been built. He has designed his own house on the property and several distinguished houses in the area for clients. What does this new habitation mean for the land? Does our looking at the landscape rather than living off of it serve it better, preserving it in a more native condition, or will our relative disconnect from the land lead us to manipulate it in new ways, for aesthetic purposes that inhibit its growth and change?

    Here, too, the Ghost projects offer an answer. They have all stood lightly on the land, adapting to the terrain and highlighting its subtleties without manipulating or aestheticizing it. The projects' site continues to serve as a cow pasture when part of it is not cordoned off for the summer construction work, an example of how we might think of the land in more multifunctional and ultimately more ecological ways. This flexibility has also characterized the Ghost projects themselves, evident in the structure that still stood from the summer before last. It had a long set of parallel, asymmetrical wood trusses partly covering a platform and an enclosing wall that extended out the back. Without any particular function, the structure served multiple roles this past summer: as a staging area for our tools and equipment, a place to eat lunch and rest, and a stage for the band at the closing celebration. Every site, however remote, holds the remains of those who have come before us, which we overlook at our own loss. That existing structure helped define our site and provided a visual connection between the two structures we built this summer, creating a composition of elements that have accumulated over time, as so often happens in traditional farmsteads.

Another accumulation was the pile of wood from previous Ghost projects, a mound of bleached boards that, like bones of dead animals waiting to take their place in a new skeleton, proved very useful in our project. In using these "found" materials, we pursued a very old way of designing and building. Rather than create a design and then bring materials from afar to construct it, most traditional builders worked with what they had on or near their site, adapting their designs to it. We did the same, adapting existing boards to new needs. That process of accepting and using what we were given implies not just a more environmentally friendly form of construction, recycling as much as possible, but also a more ethically challenging one, putting a check on the heroic designer in all of us.

The nightly appearance of the structures built on that site also had a lot to do with their being called Ghosts. Usually covered with some sort of translucent cladding or wood slats, and internally illuminated in some way for the final party, the Ghost structures have all ended up glowing eerily in the foggy night air of their seaside site. As such, they also recall the nighttime visions of almost every architect: the imagined buildings—all structure and light—that we see in our dreams and so rarely see in reality, amidst the myriad regulations that rule the making of architecture. I came to see these two-week Ghost projects as a kind of architectural exorcism, a chance for a group of designers

Ghost 6

Up lantern, down lantern

Precedent

Guests Thomas Fisher and Bob Benz with Brian MacKay-Lyons

and contractors to get this out of our system, to build and illuminate structures without concern for client programs, code requirements, or change orders.

That may partly explain the remarkable energy and sense of satisfaction that everyone displayed in these projects. We got to embrace the essence of architecture, the collective bringing together of materials to make space and form, free of all the other factors that affect architecture. Exercised and exorcised, we left that place newly empowered and perhaps no longer haunted by what we may never experience again.

MacKay-Lyons dubbed the two towers we built this past summer Simeon and Wilson after the last residents of the site. On the surface their similarities were striking: the two towers, flanking the long, low building from the summer before, aligned along the coastline, like two triumphal columns looking out to the mouth of the LaHave or two virtual lighthouses looking across to a real lighthouse on the opposite shore. The two towers also consisted of identical materials: log poles at each corner as their primary load-bearing structure, platform or balloon framing as their secondary structure, and wood slats as their exterior skin. Finally, the two buildings had the same overall form: square in plan, vertical in elevation, with flat tops and solid corners, they stood like a child's image of towers, stripped of all specific references or ornamentation.

But beneath their apparent similarities were subtle, but important, differences. One difference occurred in their location on the land. As you approached the site down the road, you first saw one tower, with the other hidden by trees, and then, after a turn in the road, you saw the other, with the first one obscured. Finally, as you arrived at the site, both towers and the structure in between came into view. As in so much of MacKay-Lyons's work, apparently simple structures can reveal remarkable complexity through their placement in and visibility from the landscape, suggesting that architects often try too hard to make their buildings dramatic, overlooking the dynamism that occurs naturally as we approach and move through them. The two towers, while similar in plan, also had very different vertical dimensions, with one standing at the top and the other at the bottom of a nearly imperceptible slope. The architecture highlighted that difference in elevation, with the ground-level bench on the uphill tower aligning with an upper floor level in the downhill tower. The two towers at the bottom of the hill revealed the powerful symbiotic relationship that can occur with the careful placement of structures in the landscape.

Another difference between the two towers existed in their detailing and construction. The uphill tower, shorter in height and in some ways simpler to construct, had a platform frame supporting vertical studs, diagonal bracing, and horizontal one-by-three slats. The downhill tower, much taller, had a more complicated double-beam structure to which we attached vertical balloon-frame studs, horizontal wood whalers, and vertical one-by-four slats. The platform frame allowed for more individual activity on the job site, giving us all a place to stand and work, while the balloon frame required more collective action, with several people on different levels of scaffolding hoisting up and fastening on longer pieces of wood. No wonder platform framing has all but replaced the balloon frame in modern construction.

Differences in detailing also distinguished the two towers. The uphill tower had an asymmetrical orientation to the adjacent structure from the previous year, with a nearly closed back corner sporting a windowlike opening to the view upriver, and a much more open front corner, with the cantilevered ground-level bench placed off center to allow for a place to sit and to provide a diagonal view of the stage. The downhill tower had, in contrast, a symmetrical organization, with closed sidewalls and ground-floor openings, in line with the uphill tower, that let the land pass under and through the building toward the sea. That tower had a similar sidewall extension at its top, showing how symmetry can have its own very dynamic quality by directing space and views.

The illumination of the two towers highlighted their differences as well. The uphill tower focused its internal lighting down, using the platform framing to create a solid ceiling that doubles as a light reflector. The downhill tower, with its upward-extending walls, directed the internal light up, creating a beacon that accentuates the height of the building. Again, as in so many of MacKay-Lyons's designs, the two towers demonstrated how much complexity arises out of simplicity. Too much of what gets built today overlooks the richness that comes from keeping most things the same. No variety exists when everything varies.

For all of the architectural lessons present in these two towers, personal lessons also arose from their construction. Four hundred years ago, when the French first arrived, few architects existed. People, of course, still designed and built structures, but those tasks existed as part of a continuum, with designers working as or alongside builders. But, after a century during which designing and building have become separate and all-too-often-adversarial activities, those two tasks have begun to come together again, driven in part by computer design and manufacturing but perhaps more significantly by our changing perception and growing suspicion of all attempts to separate related tasks and partition off parts of reality. These Ghost projects, like other design-build efforts at Dalhousie and in schools of architecture across North America, represented a profound shift in the self-perception of architects and in the education of architectural students.

Although designed by the participants, with the guidance of MacKay-Lyons, the construction of the two towers involved

Ghost 6

Balloon framing

Wilson

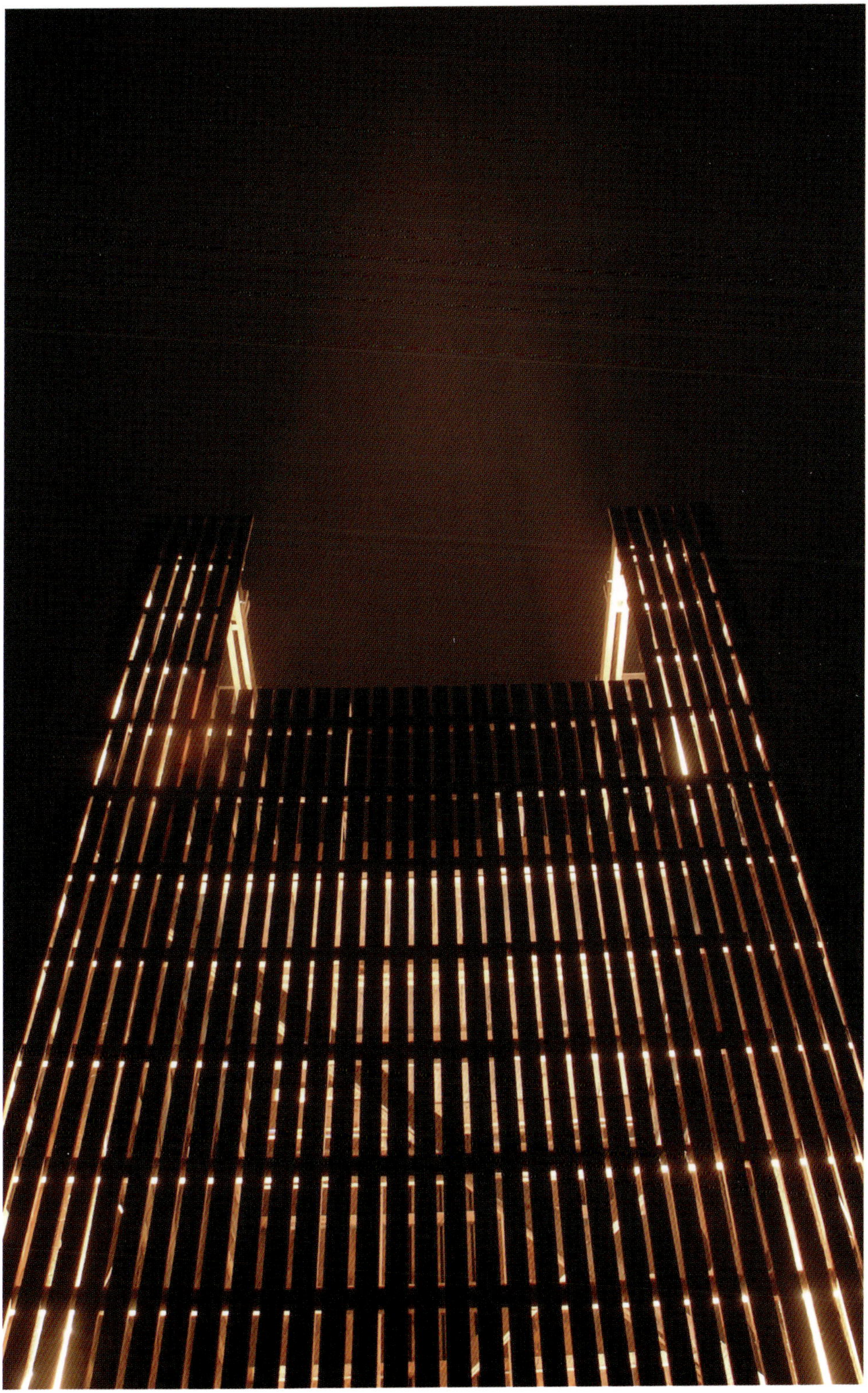

students and professionals, architects and builders, young and old. Some of the details changed as the towers went up, with everyone involved in the construction convening on-site to resolve any problems. Such is the way building has occurred through most of human history, and how it still occurs in remote places to this day. It is also the way in which building will increasingly occur around the globe, even as we face pressures to mass-produce architecture to lower its cost and increase its availability. Remaining removed from the phenomenon of mass production or thinking we must protect our professional turf in the face of it will only make architects irrelevant. Rather, by helping build what we design and by inviting builders into the design process—as in the making of these two towers—the differences and complementary knowledge of designers and builders become more apparent and mutually valued.

Our acquisition of knowledge also becomes more focused. We are faced with far more ideas, images, and information than ever before, which connect us to others even as it distances us from ourselves. In architecture this has led some to argue that the field has more to do with the flow of information and the fluidity of form than it does with the actual making of something physical or even inhabitable. This may be an acceptable part of what architecture becomes in the future, but it has certainly distanced us from what architecture has always done—shelter people—and what architecture desperately needs to do in a world in which billions of people live in unhealthy conditions.

These two towers posit a possible antidote to such distancing. We sat on the scaffolding high in the air, holding on as the two towers swayed in the wind blowing off the ocean while trying to drive spikes through the rough-cut wood—nothing fostered a greater sense of focus, of being fully in the moment, than that experience. Architecture may be about information and image, but it is also and will always be about the most fundamental human act of fastening materials together to give us shelter from the storm.

The two towers also showed how designing and constructing something can build community. The handing up or holding down of lumber, the looking after each other up on the scaffolding, the calling out for or giving of assistance, the odd conversations had high in the air while waiting for the next task to arrive all created an incredible camaraderie among the participants. Up on the two towers, among people who mostly did not know each other two weeks earlier, a real bond developed. Even in our age of distance and distraction, communities of people can still spontaneously arise.

Brian MacKay-Lyons calls the two-week Ghost projects a "crash-course in material culture." Unlike so many of his peers, whose material culture consists of products selected from Sweets Catalog, MacKay-Lyons draws his materials and detailing largely from the simple sheds, houses, and barns of his native Nova Scotia, and in so doing, has created a compelling architecture quite different from much of what gets built in North America today. Over much of the continent, you see structures made of increasingly flimsy and ephemeral materials, with predictable and often monotonous interior spaces and extravagant and often torturous exterior ornamentation. Such architecture seeks to give owners an individual identity, which backfires when everyone tries to do the same. This trend reflects a paradox in North American culture: we stand united in our effort to stand apart from each other, conforming in our drive to be nonconformists.

MacKay-Lyons's work represents a quiet but powerful critique of this phenomenon. His architecture tries to reconnect people to the culture and traditions of the place in which they live, via the craft traditions and vernacular architecture of their communities. It is easy for such an approach to become nostalgic, producing otherwise banal buildings that simply mimic the appearance of historic structures. The far more difficult course that MacKay-Lyons has pursued involves not the rejection of modernism, but its modification by filtering it through a local culture and adapting it to local conditions. This has resulted in work that has almost the opposite characteristics of so much North American architecture: buildings with material substance, spatial dynamism, and formal restraint. The Ghost projects echo that inversion of the dominant material culture in their use of substantial materials, construction methods particular to a place, and forms so spare and simple that they have a generic and almost universal appeal.

We tend to see modernism as the antithesis of traditional cultures, as a decided break from the past and old ways of being. And we typically associate modernism with individual expression and mass production, the very combination that has come to define the architectural vernacular of our time. But the work of MacKay-Lyons and the Ghost projects suggest otherwise. Both abstractly modern and culturally rooted, his architecture undermines the apparent opposition between the two and highlights their often-overlooked commonality: the desire to live lightly on the land, to see change as an inevitable part of life, and to view freedom arising from a reduction of one's material possessions. Of all the lessons learned on the Ghost projects, those might be the most profound.

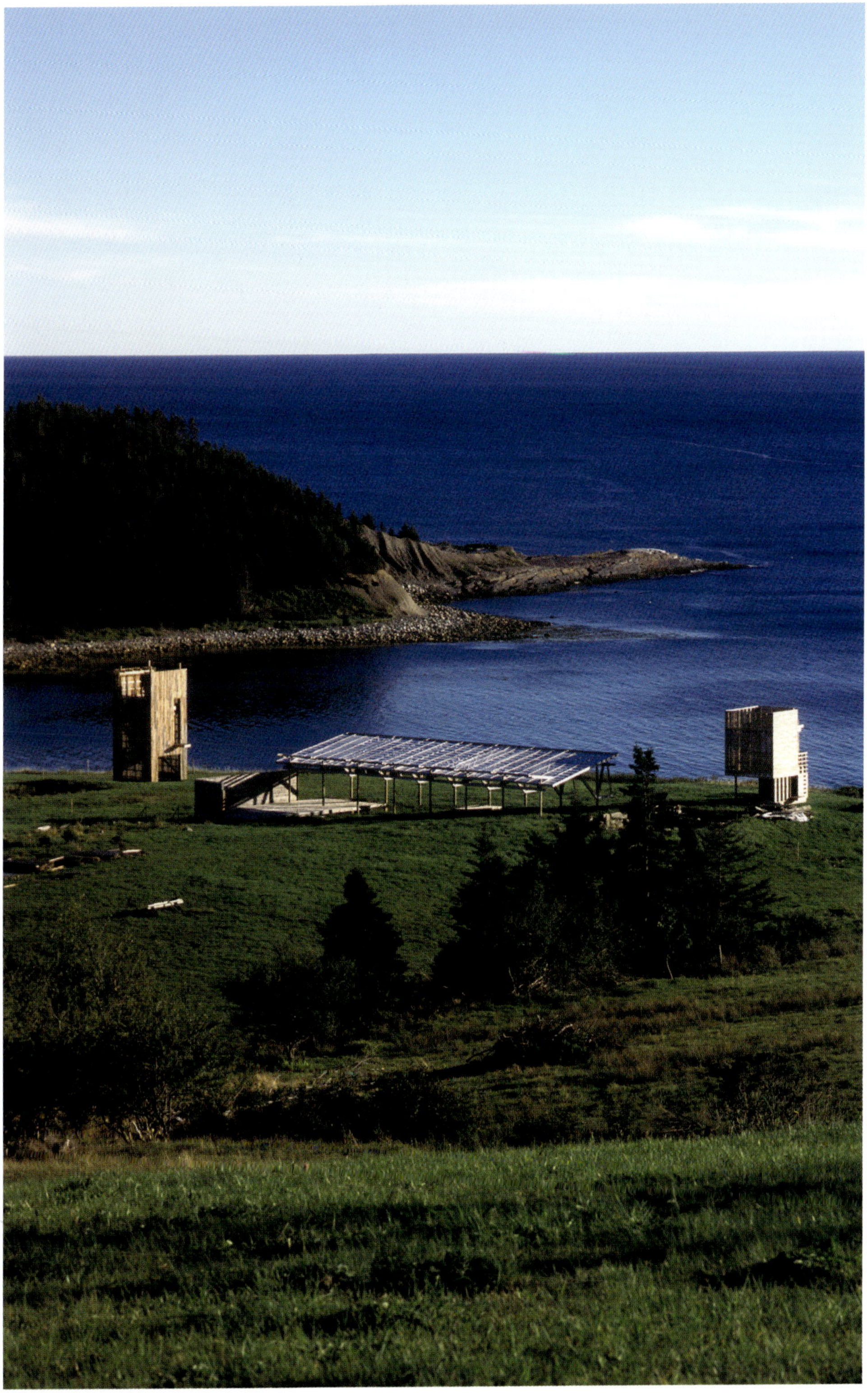

Simeon

Simeon and Wilson

The original drawing board

The Education of an Architect

Ideas say it only in things.
—William Carlos Williams

The Ghost Lab is a critique of the current state of architectural education—of both the role of practice and of the academy in teaching the discipline of architecture. It is based on the view that there is but one world. Thinking and doing, the mind and body are necessarily connected.

Current architectural practice has largely shirked its responsibility to provide meaningful apprenticeship to students and young architects. Practices have become increasingly mercenary, viewing interns as little more than a migrant labor pool. The apprenticeship model of architectural education—its roots in the master-builder tradition of the Middle Ages—offers project-based learning, an independent body of knowledge, a hierarchy based on merit, and a democratic ethos. This democratization of knowledge—which led to the emergence of the middle class—was independent from both the church and the aristocracy and must not be confused with the simplistic relativism that pervades Western society today.

The Architectural Academy has lost its connection to the physical world, becoming progressively esoteric. The disconnect between head and hand in many architectural schools has been exacerbated by an increasing reliance on virtual media and the predominance of pseudo-intellectualization. It is difficult to simulate many of the fundamental lessons of design in a virtual environment or even the classroom. (The understanding that comes from deflecting a two-by-ten rafter with one's own body weight thirty feet in the air, for example, is not something that can be taught—it can only be experienced.) The computer cannot communicate the intentionality or the speculative nature of gestural mark-making with a pencil on paper or on a plank. At the same time, university-level tenure and promotions committees impose the standards of the research culture of the sciences or the humanities on young architectural academics. The result is design professors with PhDs and little or no experience in drawing or in designing, let alone actually making things.

This combination is a recipe for disaster. A priesthood has been created by those who have a vested interest in mystification rather than intellectual and practical enablement. All of this in the guise of relativistic "self-discovery"—a kind of intellectual terrorism in the name of democracy and in the absence of imparted knowledge. After all, a priesthood needs mysteries, and the congregation must feel unworthy.

Intelligent young people who choose a life in architecture intuitively know that architecture is concerned with issues such as the environment, making, and community. The Ghost Lab attempts to get to them before they fully are put through the thickness-planer of architectural education, which trims their rough edges in exchange for trading in their common sense. Who says that the Academy has an exclusive claim on ideas? After all, we know that nothing is more intellectually engaging than the material world itself.

When I was a young and critical student, a wise teacher, Jim Sykes, once said to me: "Don't be one of those people who waste their energy criticizing. Make something better." So the Ghost Lab critiques through optimism rather than through complaint. One of the most valuable commodities in society is optimism; the idea of civilization is embodied in the human urge to build.

In this sense, the priesthood has another more benign guise as the keeper of hope in the face of an all-too-often-disappointing reality. A nineteenth-century writer tells the story of a group of men sharing a prison cell. The cell has one berth with a small window. The job of the oldest prisoner, who occupies this bed, was to report to the others about the state of the world outside. Each morning he would say, "The sun is shining, the sheep are in the fields." Many years later the youngest prisoner becomes the eldest, and he takes over this privileged position. The first morning he awakes, he looks out the window and sees only a blank wall. Then, he proceeds to tell the others: "The sun is shining and the sheep are grazing in the fields. All is well with the world. Things are as they should be."

Architect and professor Essy Baniassad says, "In architecture there is much to learn and little to teach, but what can be taught can be taught clearly." There is no shortage of real mysteries and no need for unnecessary mystification of the few things that can be more easily discussed. Methods taught—such as how to drive a nail into a board without splitting it or how to employ the ocean horizon as the ultimate level—are merely the gifts of a tool. A tool makes one independent and free. The individual spirit is irrepressible; it will always emerge.

Pragmatism is the best teacher; learning is accelerated by purpose. We learn best when we need to know: technology is best understood by making; sequence is best understood when there is little time; teamwork is learned quickly when there is too much to do; topography is most apparent when we set the height of the platform. We learn "ways of seeing" when we are searching for an authentic source of content. At the Ghost Lab, many of the lessons are implied, rather than taught. What is not discussed is what is most often important.

Each year a mix of students, professors, practitioners, artists comes to the Ghost Lab. Unfortunately, many young architects and students are there because they are dissatisfied with either the offices where they work or the education that they are receiving. The more senior professors or practicing architects come to further their common research interests. The invited guests (distinguished historians, architects, and builders) come for a collegial reaffirmation of shared values (I call it AA— Architects Anonymous). For a short period, we simulate the apprenticeship environment of the ancient guilds, where we teach and learn from one another according to levels of experience. The lost valley by the sea at the end of the earth is our test tube. For a moment we are like children in our sandbox, learning about the world through the discipline of playful curiosity.

Ghost 6

Albert Oxner fishing

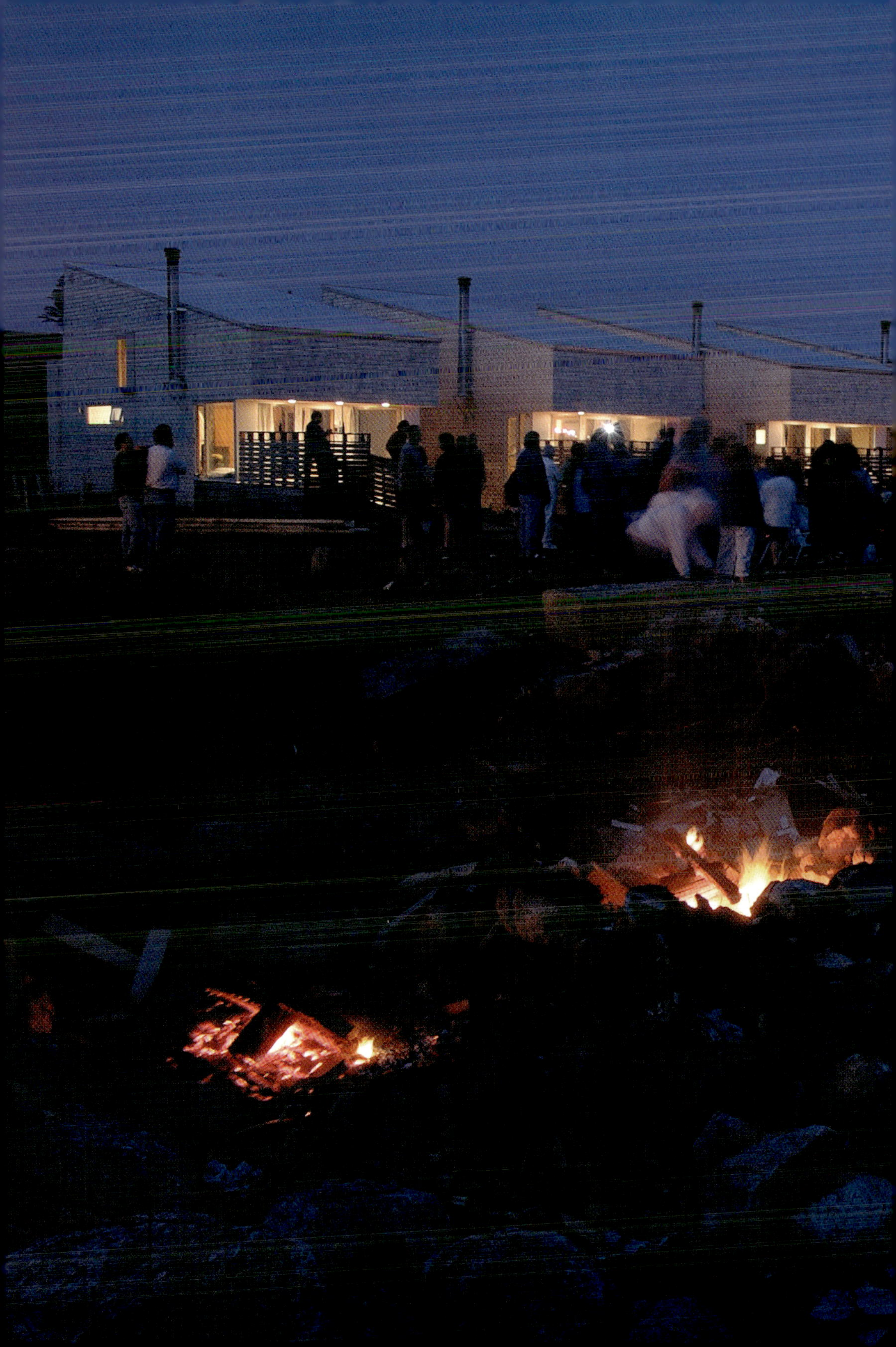

GHOST 7

July 2 to July 17, 2005

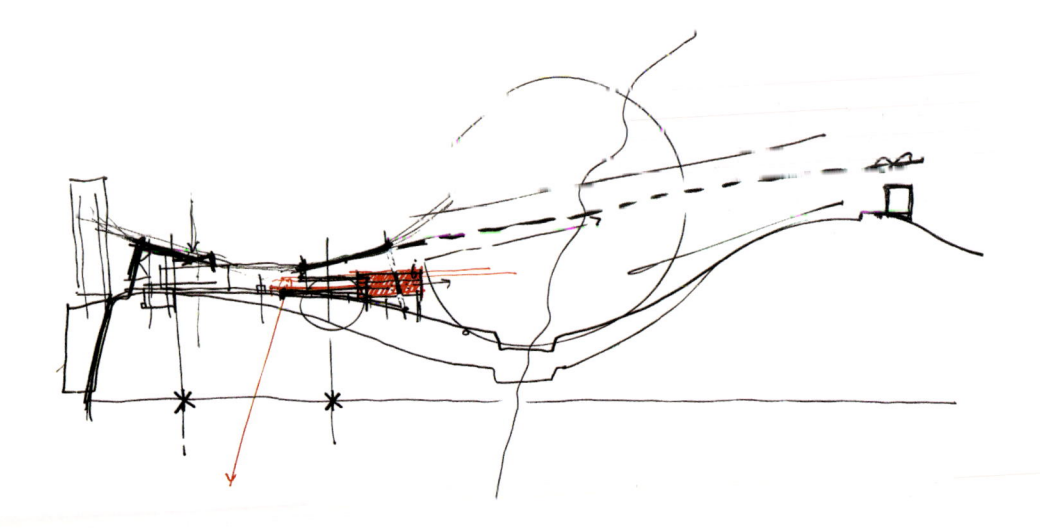

The Dance of Construction

Juhani Pallasmaa

Socrates argues in Paul Valéry's deeply moving dialogue *Eupalinos, or The Architect* (1923), a fictitious conversation between the philosopher and his friend Phaedrus, that

> Of all acts the most complete is that of constructing. A work demands love, meditation, obedience to your finest thought, the invention of laws by your soul, and many other things that it draws miraculously from your own self, which did not suspect that it possessed them. This work proceeds from the most intimate center of your existence, and yet it is distinct from yourself.[1]

The act of constructing evokes mythical perspectives. It has a double perspective: as we create a distinct place and space for human occupation, we simultaneously structure our world. Architecture also structures both the builder's and the occupant's very mind. As Gaston Bachelard appropriately observes, "House is an instrument to confront the cosmos."[2]

Every man-made structure bridges time. It turns the builder's attention simultaneously to the future and the past. The very process of building makes one think of man's earliest constructions. Every building is a first construction, and the end of the process always evokes a new beginning. The very act of constructing is not linear, it is cyclical.

Orienting the building in relation to the sun, land, and the winds, water, and views, as well as breaking into the earth,

---

1. Paul Valéry, *Dialogues*, trans. William McCausland Stewart (New York: Bollingen Foundation, 1956), 145.
2. Gaston Bachelard, *The Poetics of Space* (Boston: Beacon Press, 1969), 46.

Ghost 7

Dance

Guest architect Marlon Blackwell and guest critic Juhani Pallasmaa

Master plan on pie plate

144

collaborating with matter and gravity, balancing forces with structures and connections, constitutes a primordial rite, the dance of construction. It is also a practice of alchemy that turns blocks of stone into a wall, a piece of wood into a pillar or beam, a hole in the wall into the eye of the window, an interval of the brickwork into a doorway, and a cavity in a masonry wall into a place for fire. Human will and the skill of the builder's hand reorganize matter into a constructed thought—matter turns into an idea and a confession of faith.

Building is not primarily about providing shelter; it implies reorganizing and domesticating the nameless and the measureless, creating a domicile, and giving it a name. The elements are reconfigured through construction to create a place for occupation. An architectural structure puts us in an unforeseen and poeticized relation with the world. Just as the jar in Wallace Stevens's poem "Anecdote of the Jar" (1990) magically tames the wilderness of Tennessee hills, architectural structures redefine and rescale the landscape. A building marks the human presence in the landscape. In fact, every building creates a microcosm, a domesticated and miniaturized world.

Construction implies the projection of a silent theory and a series of evaluations that turn the structure into a manifestation of the human condition. We know and understand our world and ourselves as cultural beings primarily through our own constructions, both material and mental, past and present.

"Destroying and constructing are equal in importance, and we must have souls for the one and the other," argues Phaedrus.[3] In accordance with his observation, construction implies selection and choice. There is no construction without destruction; the very act of building always demolishes and wipes out something that has existed at the same time that it reveals and creates something new. Construction prohibits as it permits,

---

3. Valéry, *Dialogues*, 70.

restricts as it emancipates, closes as it opens. The innocence of the landscape is forever lost through the act of human construction. An architect's greatness is measured by the capacity and skill to balance these opposite processes of annihilation and creation. The architect's true talent arises from an intensified sense of reality, not sentimental journeys of fantasy. Instead of obscuring and distracting, the task of architecture is to clarify and intensify.

"What is there more mysterious than clarity?" asks Socrates rhetorically in the Valéry dialogue.[4] Construction brings order to chaos, predictability to randomness, and meaning to meaninglessness. The order of architecture creates an instrument to measure, structure, and understand the world. As we build a structure, we also reconstruct ourselves. Houses constitute our extended bodies as well as our externalized senses, memories, and minds. The house senses, selects, and thinks on our behalf. Our most essential preunderstanding of the world arises from the historical accumulation of architectural structures.

Building implies and evokes optimism: we are able to build only to the degree that we have confidence in the future. Pessimistic or nihilistic construction is necessarily a preparation for the apocalypse. Construction also implies the projection of beliefs and ideals. We can only build as far as we attempt to build a better and more humane world.

The primordial encounter of land and water, air and fire at the Ghost site in Nova Scotia, combined with its thick sense of local history and the feeling of shared purpose brought about by collective work, made the construction laboratory a memorable experience for all of us. The rhythm of collective labor is hypnotic; the repetitious sound of work turns physical labor into a shared performance, a dance that carries itself forward without apparent effort. The collective flow of work builds on

---

4. Ibid., 107.

Ghost 7

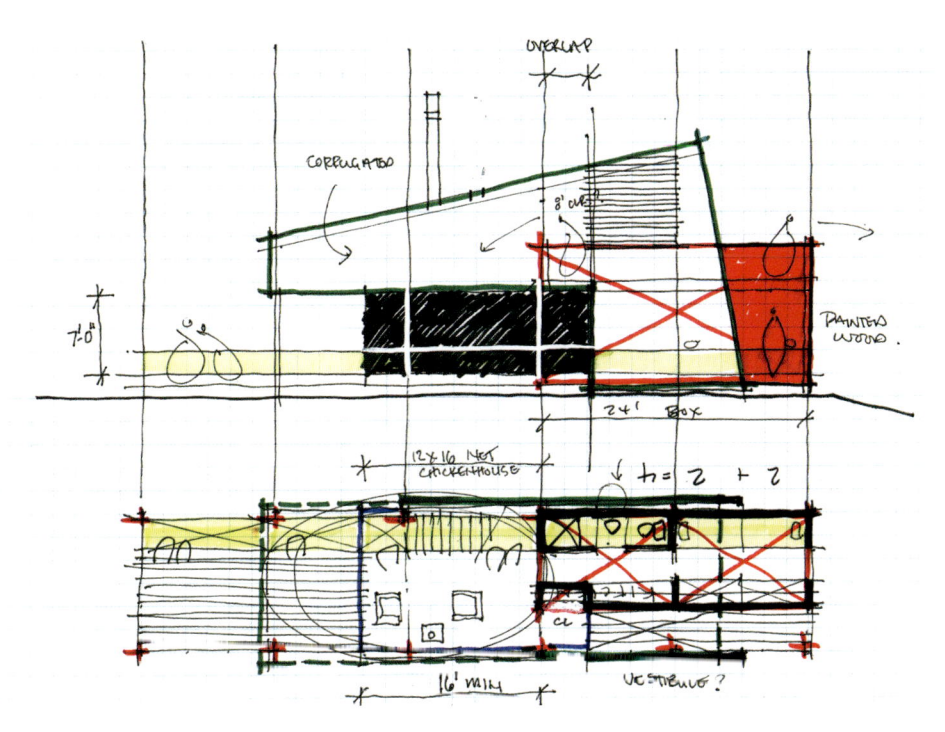

Cabin sketches

Ghost 7

Raising

Ghost 7

Minimum

Sequence   Bite

Ghost 7

Box and sleeve

The Bluenose Fiddlers

itself and completes itself. Diligence and the rhythm of work are contagious. The body and the hand of the maker fuse work and thought into a singular action. Construction both fatigues and rejuvenates, humbles and makes one proud. The aching fatigue after a day of hard physical labor is extraordinarily therapeutic and emancipatory.

Joseph Brodsky, the Nobel laureate poet, makes the following comment on the role of craft in writing poetry:

> No honest craftsman or maker knows in the process of working whether he is making or creating…The first, the second, and the last reality for him is the work itself, the very process of working. The process takes precedence over its result, if only because the latter is impossible without the former…In reality (in art and, I would think, science), experience and the accompanying expertise are the maker's worst enemies.[5]

In the architect's and builder's work, likewise, the process and the product, the idea and its materialization, the maker and the object are inseparably merged. Regardless of our overt intentions, we are always bound to build our self-portrait. After the joy and trance of the process of making, however, the quality of the product is its sole justification.

The closing party of the Ghost workshop in the darkness of the Nova Scotian night, illuminated by the forceful campfire in the scale of a natural phenomenon that devoured all the remains of the construction work, felt like an ancient rite of propitiating the gods. We all floated and swam in the magical liquid of darkness and music, until the last flames of fire and notes of music died away in the silence beneath the immense firmament of Nova Scotia.

---

5. Joseph Brodsky, "A Cat's Meow," *On Grief and Reason: Essays* (New York: Farrar, Straus, and Giroux, 1997), 301.

Ghost 7 was the first permanent Ghost project. It provides lodging for future Ghost participants—an optimistic vision of longevity for the project and for the site. While offering refuge in the landscape, Ghost 7 is a perforated, less-defensive version of the archetypal courtyard form of habitation. As a result, the landscape percolates through the scheme. The siting geometry is drawn from the structural grid of the Ghost 5 project opposite.

The four resulting structures can be described both as cabins and as pavilions. They are cabins by way of their limited size (720 square feet) and their modest means; they are pavilions by way of their ambition to create a rich range of spatial experience within a modernist free plan within the landscape. The series of Ghost 7 buildings, with tight spaces between, is based on the precedent of a collection of a particular, yet typical, group of closely spaced Nova Scotian fish sheds.

In the manner of Louis Kahn, the parti consists of a "servant box," wrapped by a larger "served shed." The servant box contains the sleeping areas, bathroom, kitchen, mechanical services, and balcony; the served shed houses the gathering space. The box is a finished and heated retreat clad in vertical boards while the shed remains raw and unheated and clad in eastern white shingles four inches to the weather.

The post foundations result in a minimum impact on the land. Prefabricated built-up wood trusses at twelve feet on center form the primary structure, which focuses the loads into the foundations. The envelope consists of a rough-sawn wood two-by-four stud frame. The metal roofing is corrugated Galvalume.

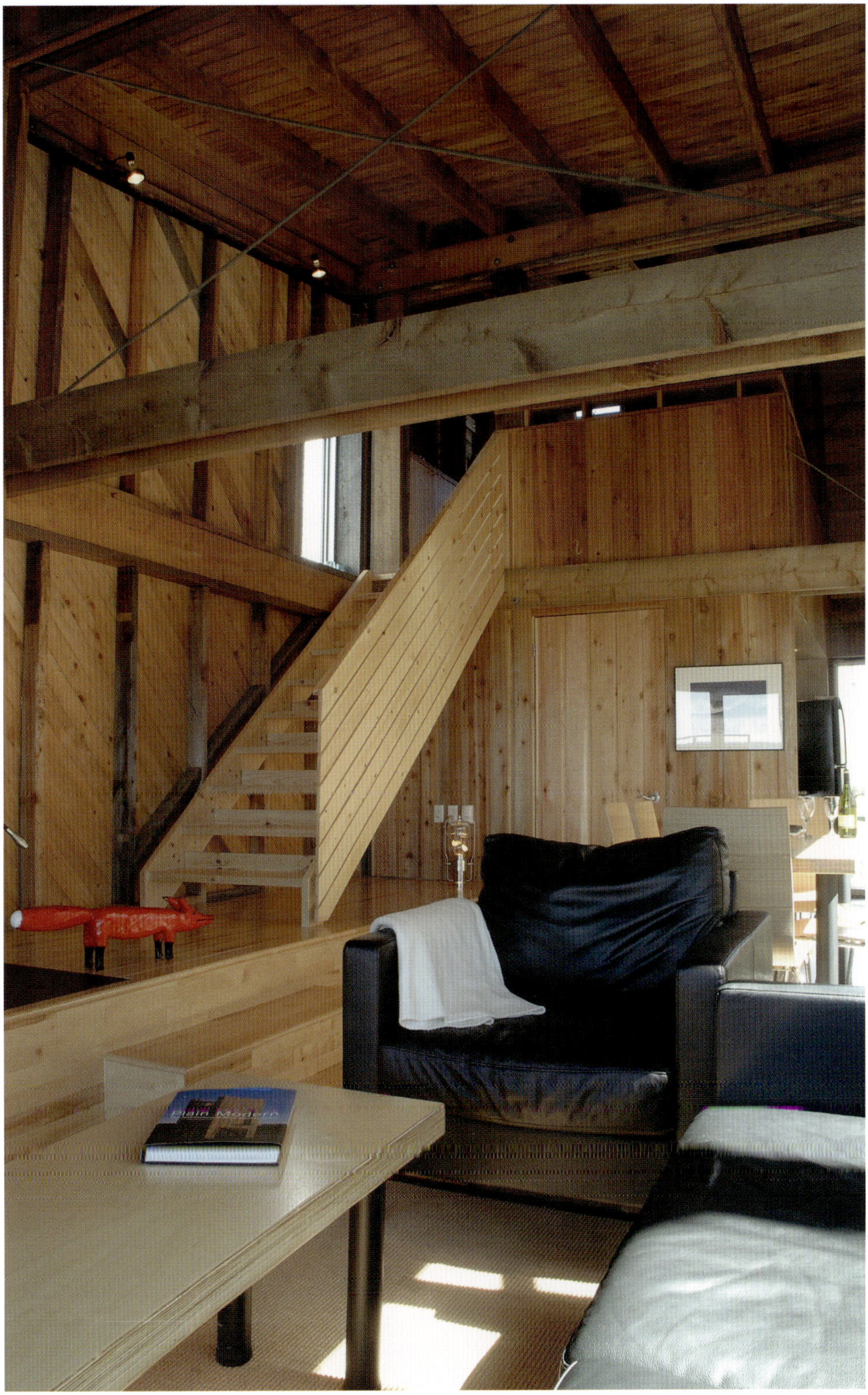
Plain Modern

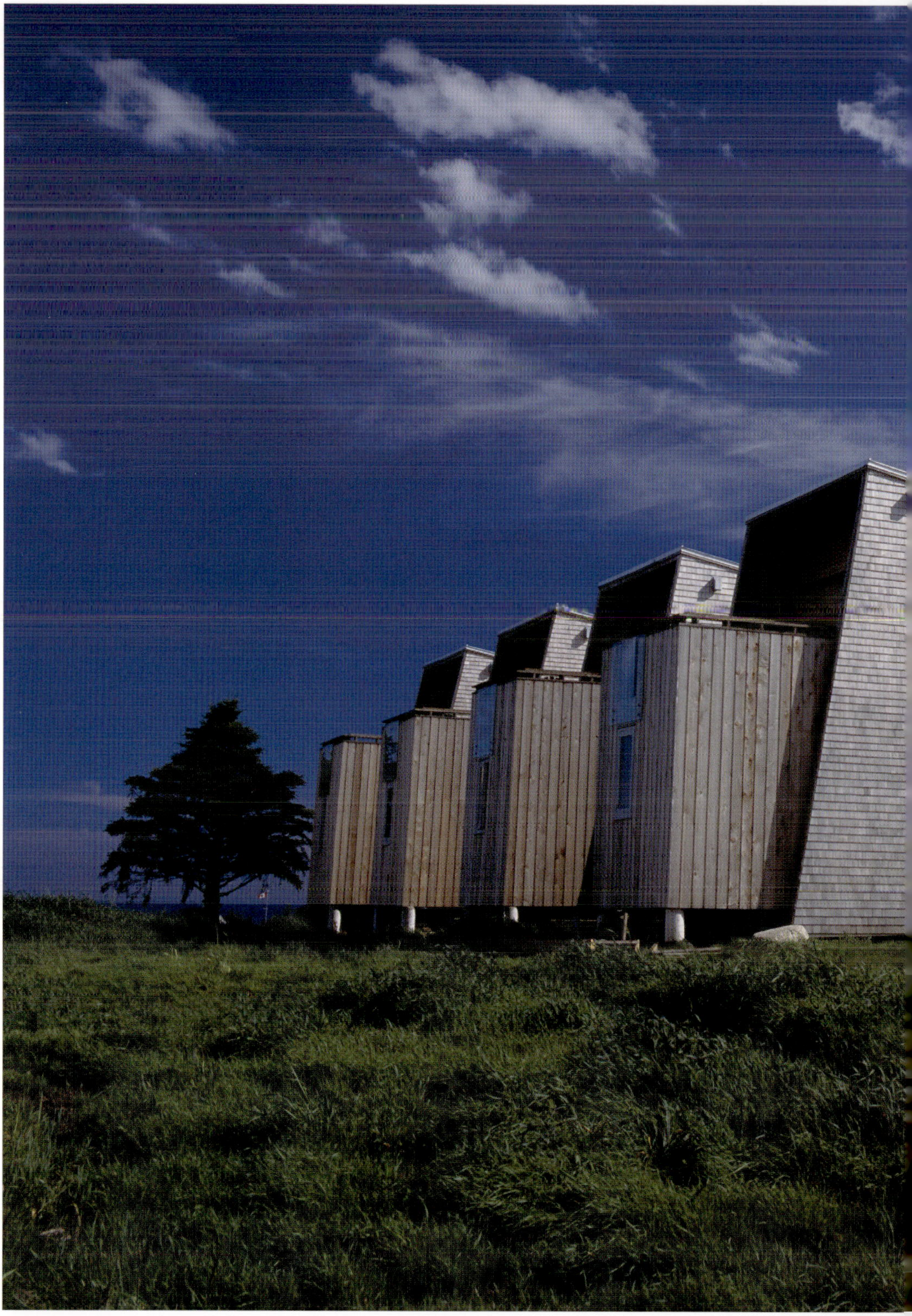

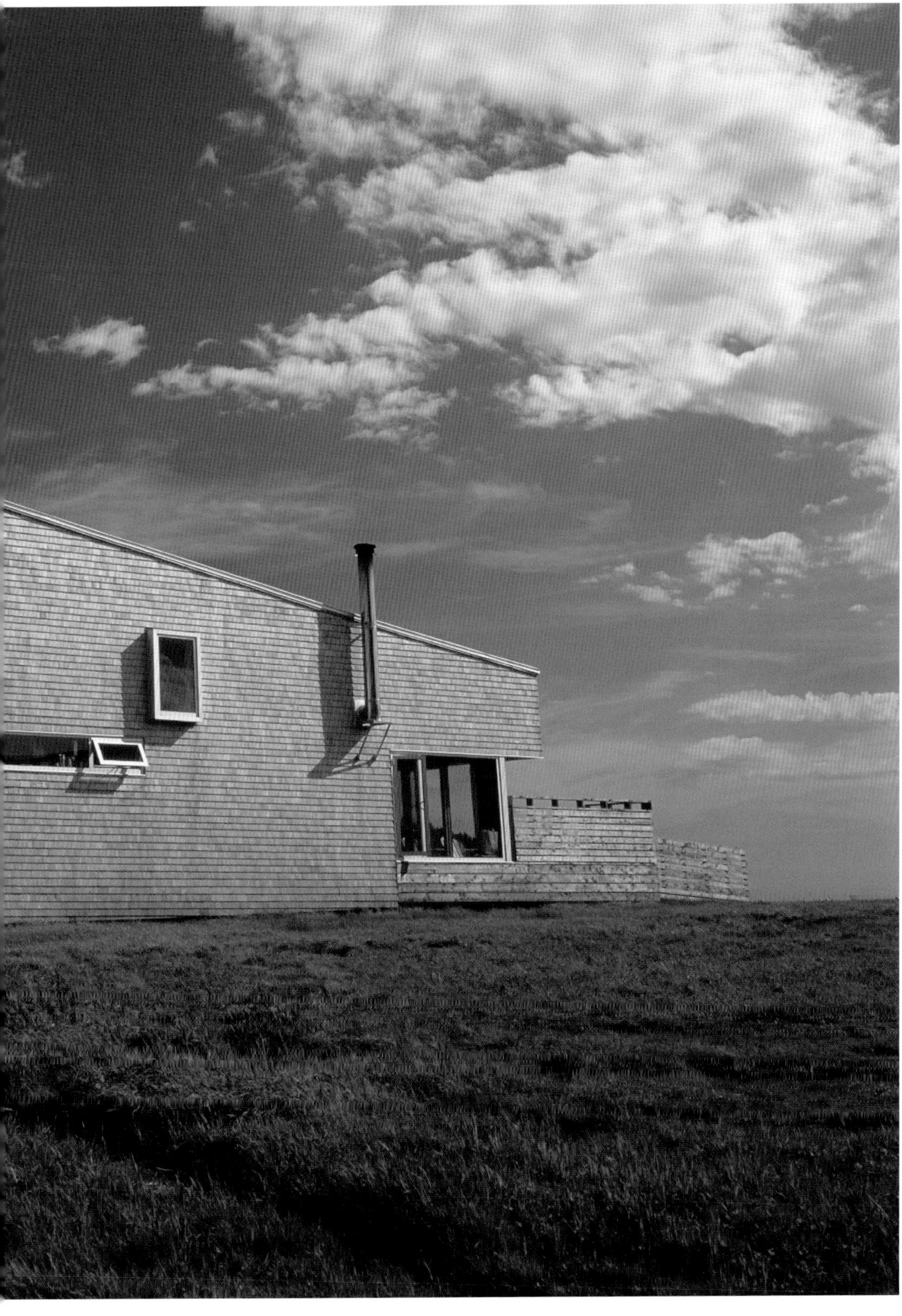

Gathering sea-manure

Village Architect

Perhaps, despite our globalized world, this is still the mythic stuff of which some kind of cultural resistance may yet be enjoined.
—Kenneth Frampton

One day when I was four years old, my brother and I attempted to reach around a classical column in the Roman Forum. From that moment on, I knew I was going to be an architect. Even now, when I go to the mountain, I am moved by the masterworks of architecture—like Dorothy in *The Wizard of Oz*, I remind myself, "There's no place like home." Back in the village of Arcadia, Nova Scotia, I dreamt of practicing architecture one day like a country doctor, making house calls in rural communities, making a contribution to the quality of my native landscape. This would not be the typical slash-and-burn practice, where one gets to escape one's creations, but rather a practice where you live among your buildings, and you wear your body of work. On returning to Nova Scotia after living abroad in Japan, Tuscany, and Los Angeles, my wife and I bought a farm in the village of Upper Kingsburg on Nova Scotia's Atlantic coast. Here we put down roots, brought up our children—and I have become its village architect.

Ghost 7

This village landscape is an experimental laboratory, or a sandbox, for MacKay-Lyons Sweetapple Architects. It is a place to study culture, where each architectural commission becomes part of a larger environmental work-in-progress, where stewardship takes precedence over architectural fashion.

Now, some patients who come to the country doctor have a cold and need to take two aspirin and go to bed. Others need brain surgery. So we make both background and foreground buildings for the village clients/patients. Background buildings, which bear a closer resemblance to vernacular prototypes, contribute almost invisibly to the modest fabric of the place. The foreground projects are more overtly modern. Both the rustic and the refined, the figurative and the abstract, however, share a common quality of simplicity. We might call it plainness, or we might call it minimalism. This quality connects both the highbrow and the lowbrow and results in a sense of timelessness. A democratic imperative drives us toward the view of one world—not one for the cognoscenti and another for everyone else. When you have to live in the landscape with your projects, you ask yourself whether it is the unique work of art or the good generic that make the better built landscape. While working in a place with a strong and well-established character, one must avoid both historicist pastiche and a blind, modernist belief in progress.

And who are these village clients? In a few cases they are local folks. Many are artists of one sort or another (painters, graphic designers, filmmakers, photographers, authors). Most are newcomers who need an architectural Seeing Eye dog to introduce them to the place. Most have become friends. The client group also includes the elders who have passed on—the ancestors—and the children yet to be born. In fact, the whole community is involved and does not hesitate to cast judgment about what fits and what does not. When an architect is part of a community, it is not clear whether it is the building, the architect, or the building's inhabitants that are tolerated by the locals. Respect becomes more important than taste.

The Italian architect Giancarlo de Carlo often said, "To serve is not to be a servant." This is the nature of a critical-regionalist position within society. One must first have empathy for a place, the clients, the users, the community. But it is not enough to replicate what is or what once was or even simply produce what is asked for. The village architect must sustain a critical position within society. The architectural result in the area of the Ghost site is absolute modernity that, at the same time, acknowledges cultural continuity.

Architecture is a social art. If the practice of architecture is the art of what you can make happen, then you are only as good as your bullpen—the builders, the engineers, the artisans, the colleagues, the staff—that collaborates with you and is possessed by the same urge to build, by the same belief that the project is something exceptional. It is the local builders, carpenters, and ship-builders who have taught me about the nature of materials, about labor, about how climate affects buildings, and about how construction sequence influences design decisions—in short, everything that I did not learn about technology in architecture school.

I have learned that construction is a verb. It is about process, view and cultural ways and means. Structure is a noun more static, more absolute, less relative. In the design process, the builder plays the role of the verb, and the structural engineer is the noun. It is the interplay between these two ideas, or the dialogue between building and structure, that makes each project a unique answer to the question, "How did this building get here?" For the village architect, it is the "design" of the community of collaborators that, in turn, enables the production of specific buildings. That is the real design project.

The village architect is like a farmer who is engaged in cultivation rather than consumption of the land. My wisest neighbor, Albert Oxner, like all of the farmers in the village, would take his team of oxen down to the beach each year after spring storms to gather the sea-manure that had washed up onto the shore. He would then plough it into the land to improve the soil. In doing this he left his world a little better than he had found it.

Over a number of years, MacKay-Lyons Sweetapple Architects has added many buildings to the village around the Ghost site. This aggregation of projects by a single firm in one place is relatively unique in our modern, mobile world. This constant tilling into the same soil creates a kind of quiet intensity, a considerable, focused investment. As the firm moves outward from the village to the larger world, there is an attempt to replicate this kind of aggregation of projects, whether the context is an urban neighborhood or a university campus. In each situation it is the protourban conversation between both new and exciting projects over time that takes precedence over the individual building as an independent object.

The Ghost Lab is simply an extension of the village architect's research. Like the other projects in the village, each Ghost project is a study about a particular question: how the wind can spiral through a tube (Ghost 3), for example, or how a community place can be made between two towers (Ghost 6). These questions play a didactic role in teaching about the landscape, building, and community. The Ghost concert, which consummates the completion of each year's Ghost, is simply another way of contributing to the community, of putting something back into the soil. The musicians and the local community show up out of a natural curiosity for architecture, and for one night each year, the ghost village comes back to life like the apparition of a burning ship on the ocean horizon.

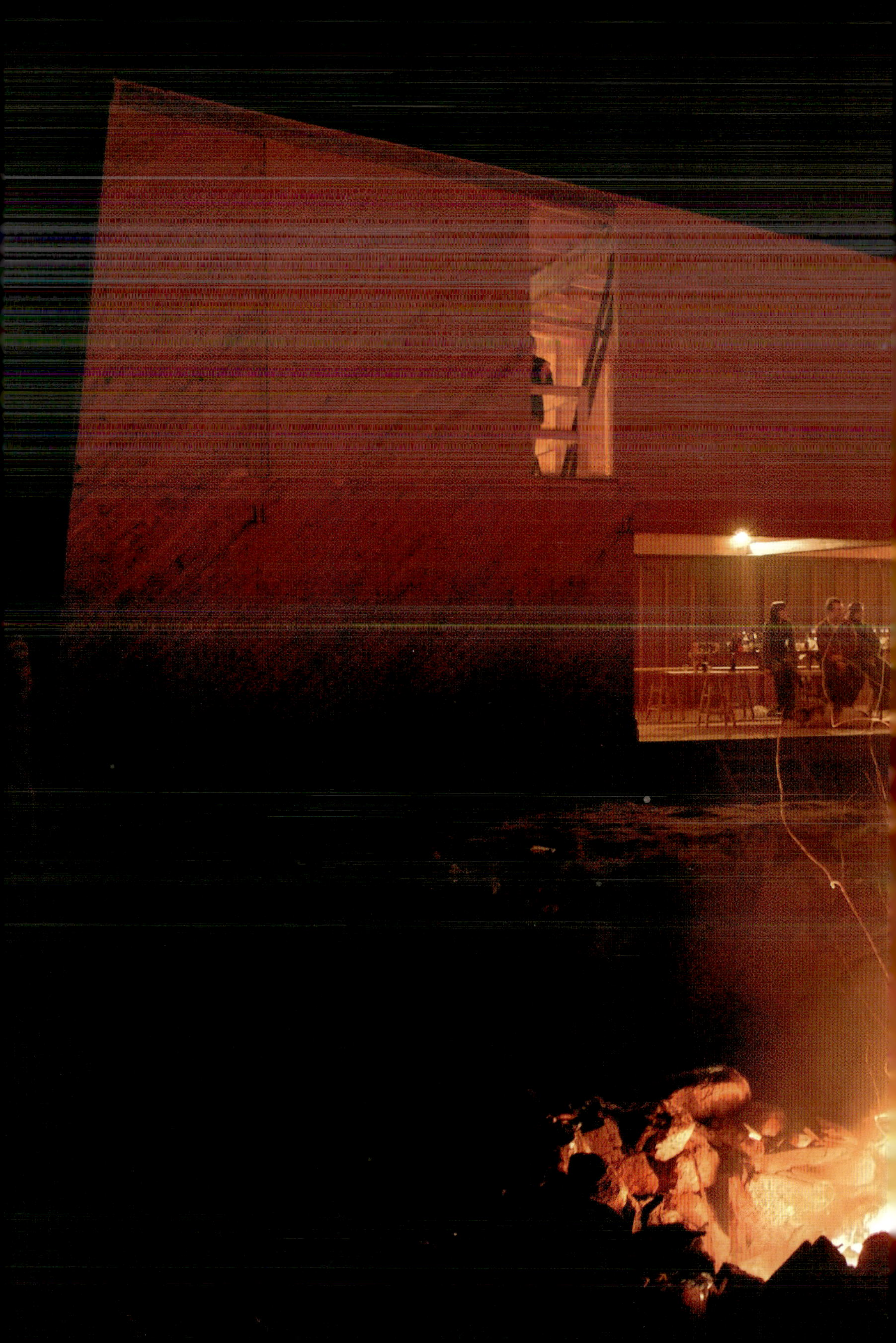

GHOST 8

July 1 to July 15, 2006

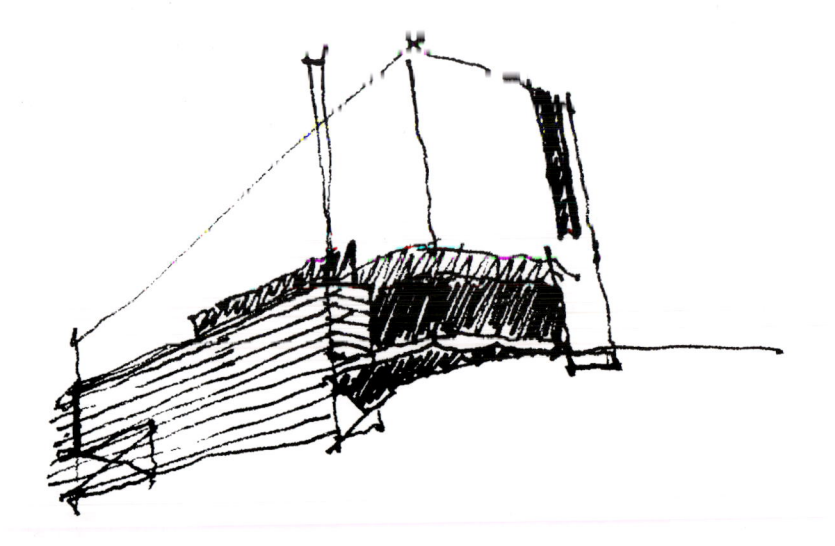

Escaping Normality
to Embrace Reality

Peter Buchanan

Precursors of Ghost 8, Ghosts 1 through 6 created temporary structures of fairly notional functionality. As well as being a very physical, hands-on immersion in materials and construction, designing and building offered lessons in the evocative engagement with the wondrous surrounding landscape and the remnants of earlier structures—both previous student exercises and the vestigial traces of a long-abandoned settlement. The spectral presence of Ghost 6's twin towers that looms spookily in the frequent fog and the misty memories of early settlers are some of the ghosts referred to by the name of the series. Ghost 7 resulted in the design and partial erection of four wedge-shaped cabins. These were completed for use by Ghost 8, which added to it a large shed—nominally a barn—intended for later conversion into a studio to be used for Ghost Lab and as a satellite office for MacKay-Lyons Sweetapple Architects.

The memorable success of Ghost 8 arose from factors that could be seen as offering two broad contrasts. One was between the magnificence of Ghost 8's attractions and the extreme constraints that also applied. The other was that the escape from the narrow normalities of academe and practice into rural isolation did not lead to a detachment from reality but to an embracing of both more physically tangible realities and larger—even somewhat mythic—ones than typically engaged with by students and architects.

As well as the sense of achievement once it was over, the most magnificent aspect of Ghost 8 was the splendor of the set-

Ghost 8

Northwest view

Platform-frame envelope structure

Barn design session

ting. The site is a meadow where the land flattens out between a grassy ridge that rolls down to it from the east and a small cliff descending to the wide, island-dotted LaHave estuary to the west. The views of the estuary are enhanced by the foreground framing of the Ghost 6 towers while to the south is a fine view of the Atlantic, its beaches, and headlands. Splendid, too, if then somewhat crowded by students, are the cabins (ever-present reminders of the quality achieved by the previous Ghost). Finally there was the climactic concert during which a large gathering of locals came to see and celebrate the new structure to music by local musicians, some of international repute.

  The fellow participants were an attraction, too—meeting and collaborating with a range of somewhat like-minded apprentice architects as well as encountering and learning from, in the manner of an apprenticeship, the more experienced architects and builders guiding the event. Prime among the latter was MacKay-Lyons. Though abstractly modern, his architecture has deep roots in place and past, in vernacular forms and traditional construction. Besides enhancing a sense of local identity and belonging, a simple directness of form and expressed construction brings its own aesthetic satisfactions.

  Two of those helping MacKay-Lyons were long-term collaborators: Bob Benz, now based in California, had worked with MacKay-Lyons for many years and is an immensely experienced builder as well as architect; local contractor Gordon MacLean has built many MacKay-Lyons buildings. Both combine an inventive pragmatism with an energetic enthusiasm that makes them natural teachers. From Seattle came David Miller, who like MacKay-Lyons is a professor and whose distinguished practice, Miller | Hull Partnership, tends to also be classified as regionalist. And I joined from London.

  The tight constraints proved far from crippling. The most pressing was shortage of time: a mere fortnight in which to work up a rough design, resolve all issues of construction and detailing, and then erect the shell of a hundred foot long building that is two stories high at one end. Crucial decisions had to be taken and preparations made prior to the participants' arrival: the building's purpose finalized and the location, orientation, plan dimensions, and the spacing of the primary structural bays determined so that concrete foundations were cast and waiting.

Time pressure and the need to make quick decisions and readily endorse the contribution of others, so as to get on with construction as soon as possible, all helped forge the strong spirit of collaboration that characterized Ghost 8. This was a group of team players that accepted and made the most of each other's strengths and skills and understood that working together is as much a creative process as prima donna self-expression. Other constraints were those of the cost and immediate availability of materials, the relatively limited building skills and experience of most of the group, the limited range of tools and technology on-site, and the need to ensure safety. This was a low-tech site, without even the most primitive of hoisting equipment. But this further ensured that everybody could play their part and learn that limited means are no constraint to creativity and achievement.

Gathering on a remote rural site to collaborate in building at great speed in a low-tech fashion with local materials was undoubtedly a respite from the norms of academe and practice. It was the antithesis of both literary-derived theories and "paper projects" of solo students (aspirant lone geniuses) in which, especially since the advent of digital technologies, seemingly anything is possible in terms of form and construction. It also differs from the slower rhythms of practice where designs tend to be developed and executed in a disengaged fashion on the computer and over the telephone and where the bureaucratic

Ghost 8

Steel-to-wood connection in primary structure

Bob Benz, Brian MacKay-Lyons, and David Miller

Guest critic Peter Buchanan with
Brian MacKay-Lyons

Lennie Gallant

processes can drag on dishearteningly. Many participants have said the real appeal of Ghost was an intense immersion in what they found lacking in their education and early years in practice.

Escaping these norms was to engage a more immediate, very physical reality, the whole experience intensified by the already mentioned constraints of time, budget, technology, and tools. These constraints tend to be little discussed in architectural education, but in practice are crucial determinants of design that should be considered in any critical appraisal. Other ever-present realities, especially because of living on-site, were the landscape and climate—the former constantly changing in mood with the latter and, in turn, affecting every experience of the participants. (Again, architecture must anticipate and respond to these changing moods as well as the weathering and patination they bring.) Ghost is a very physical learning experience, involving cold wind and rain or blazing sun, tramping in mud or clambering up scaffolding, hoisting materials or wielding and guiding tools. Participants gain more than intellectual knowledge about construction but acquire that all-important feel for its materials and processes, as well as an understanding of the need to always consider the sequencing and safety of the latter.

Beyond the intimate engagement with physical realities, Ghost also touched on almost-mythic memories that can shape and root architecture. Nova Scotia was one of the first parts of North America to be settled by Europeans continuously over time. It was originally settled by the French, whose Acadian descendents remain there and from whom MacKay-Lyons is descended. They, and later settlers and fishermen, adopted patterns of inhabitation and methods of construction—many adapted from the craft of boat building—that MacKay-Lyons keeps in mind as he designs and builds.

If anything seemed unreal about Ghost, it was the speed with which it proceeded. This pace would be impossible in most of the developed world, where gaining planning permissions and passing building regulations are arduous, long-term processes, and where deliveries of even standard materials take time. A major advantage of Ghost taking place in Nova Scotia—in MacKay-Lyons's rural "backyard"—was the relationship of mutual trust and collaboration he has built up with regulatory authorities and materials suppliers.

Although all participants contributed to and can feel some ownership of the result, Ghost 8 is a MacKay-Lyons Sweetapple Architects building, owned by Brian and used by the firm, part of its oeuvre and very identity. But as in any good architectural practice, the contributions of others were welcomed if they elaborated or refined, rather than contradicted or muddied, the evolving spirit of the design. This way of working recalls that of apprenticeship, the traditional way architecture was learned and still is in the crucial years immediately after graduating.

The building is immediately recognizable as being by MacKay-Lyons Sweetapple Architects—one of a series of wedge-shaped buildings designed as conspicuous yet complimentary counterpoints to the landscape. One of the earliest of these structures, the Messenger House, overlooks the Ghost site. Its simple, strong form rises as an emphatic, stabilizing counterthrust to the downward slope of the ridge it crests, so that the relatively small structure commands site and setting. Ghost 7's neat row of cabins are also wedges, but though they rise counter to the slight slope of the ground, the form anticipates and signals a relationship to the slope up to the ridge behind them. Larger and less articulated than the cabins, and clad in a corrugated steel sheet contrasting with their wood shingles, the

Ghost 8

Building as landscape

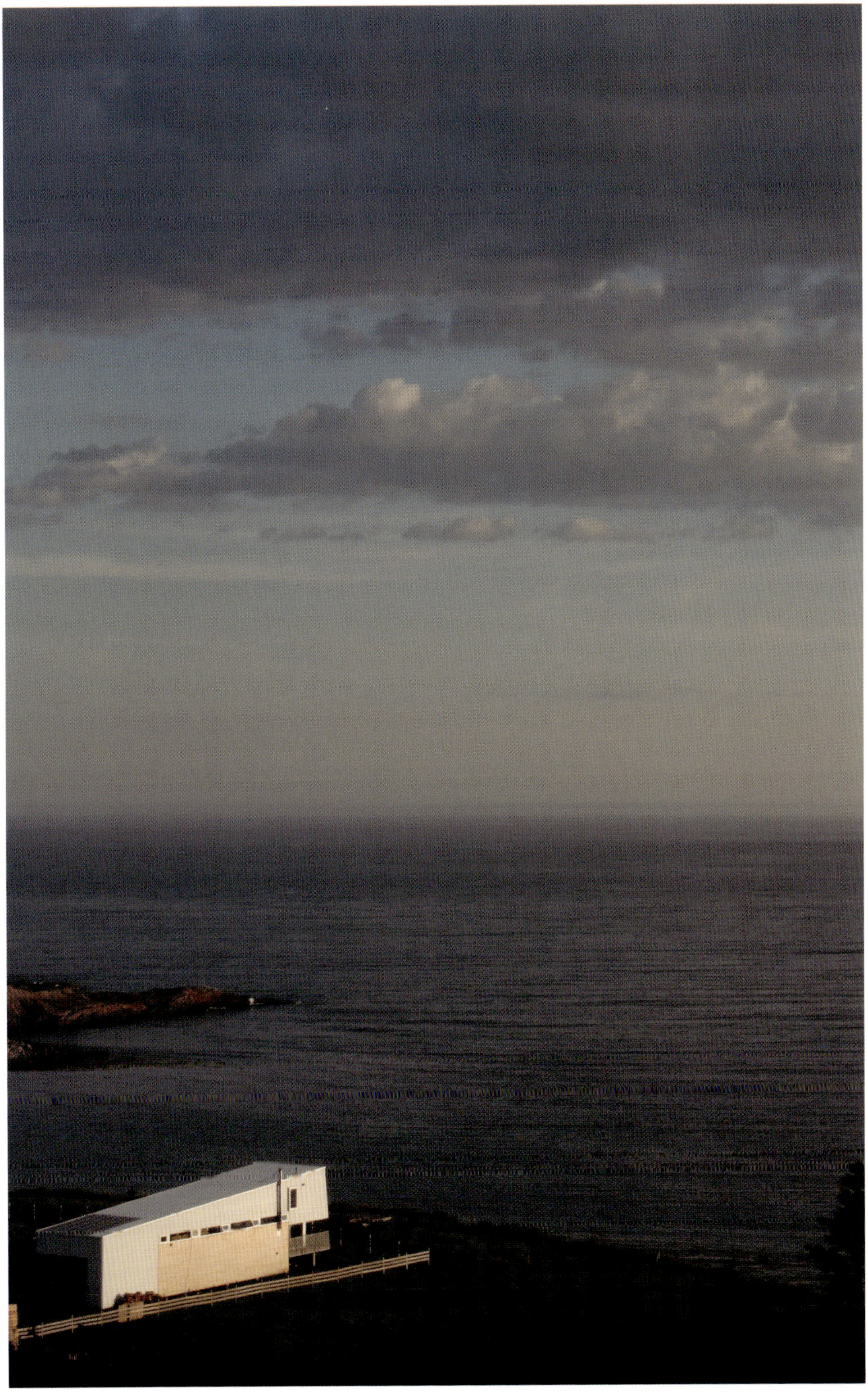

figure of Ghost 8 rises in counterpoint to the cabins while also announcing the edge of the land, the steeply sloping end wall anticipating the cliff just beyond it. The building thus interacts as part of a family of forms with the Messenger House and the cabins, the ensemble forming a larger whole in harmony with the landscape that it both fits into and takes possession of.

    This formal logic may seem watertight. But MacKay-Lyons's wife, Marilyn, was unsure, wondering if people might misunderstand and see her husband as in a creative rut. So one group discussion during design development thoroughly reappraised the design and looked quickly at some potential alternatives before collectively reaffirming its aptness. This proved important in giving everybody a chance to "buy in" to the design, and in prompting some timely reflections.

    Modern architecture's underpinning myth that each design should arise *de novo* was naive, and its influence lingers in an overemphasis on and misunderstanding of originality. Striving merely to be different leads to freakishness and a sense of formal disconnection, and so to fragmentation and lack of belonging, as the contemporary built environment proves. Indeed, many believe real originality and depth are only possible within, or in reference to, the forms of tradition. Against these, the subtlest innovations register, advancing rather than disconnecting from a lineage that might go back to mythical origins.

    Wherever a profound harmony has been achieved architecturally, it is not merely through the use of a limited palette of local materials and common design motifs but also through the elaboration of variations on recurring types, as the nearby UNESCO World Heritage Site of Lunenburg shows. (The proximity of Lunenburg is one of the attractions of Ghost and one of the resources MacKay-Lyons uses for teaching purposes.) This does not preclude the invention of new types where appropriate, such as the wedge. MacKay-Lyons is a composer-architect who like all premodern architects elaborates variations on formal types, as much as Frank Lloyd Wright, another architect concerned with place and belonging, elaborated variations of the Prairie and Usonian house types.

Like Wright, MacKay-Lyons composes with grids, axial alignments, and pinwheeling relationships—although the last of these are found not only in plan but in elevation also—a characteristic typical of the placing of openings in Nova Scotian barns and outbuildings. Although the barn/studio of Ghost 8 is axially aligned parallel with the cabins, it is set perpendicular to the grouping of them, its low end meeting a line projecting beyond the low ends of the cabins so that together they define two edges of a grassy expanse. Most of the studio and its covered terrace face south over the grass, but a portion under a raised gallery opens onto a small L-shaped deck commanding stunning views across and up the LaHave estuary, which are especially magical at sunset. These openings are in a pinwheeling relationship to each other in plan. In elevation, other openings reach up above them to form more pinwheel relationships.

Within the wedge type, the studio's innovations and originality appear mainly in the details of its primary structural elements and the conceptually elegant, visually clean integration of its contrasting materials. Like the earlier Ghosts, the primary structural material is local timber rough sawn into standard sizes, and the primary structural elements, such as posts and beams, are made up of multiples of these. But a large single volume on this exposed and windy site built of wood alone would have required a lot of material. More sensible was to include a stiffening web of standard steel angles to take wind loads back to concrete fin walls.

Ghost 8

Dusk, studio

Dusk, interior

A typical solution would have been to create structural frames or bents and hoist these into place. But lack of hoisting equipment, the need to keep all elements of easily handled weight, and the concern for the safety of an inexperienced crew necessitated a different approach. Instead, lengths of wood and steel were prefabricated and lifted into place by hand and integrated without notching the timber or using steel gusset plates. This was achieved by using quarter-inch plywood as a slightly recessed spacer between the two-inch-wide boards. Between these were slotted the quarter-inch-thick steel tongues, created by cutting away the end of one flange of the steel angles of the web. A single bolt then secured the steel and wood together.

Detailing is really about simplification, synthesis, and systematization so that a minimal number of details repeat as often as possible, giving the design a seemingly unforced ease and clarity. The result here is especially satisfying when looking down the length of the building from the loft: the angled struts of the web get progressively longer and steeper as they approach the viewer, adding a dynamism of their own to the swelling space and proving that prosaic construction can achieve an understated poetry.

Insight into detailing is only one of many lessons offered by the Ghost experience. Others included acquiring the all-important "feel" for materials and construction as well as for the relationship between architecture, landscape, and climate. Two potential lessons are particularly timely. As buildings and the technical means of realizing them that are now drawn on during both design and construction become ever more complex, architects must work ever closer with consultants and contractors in eliciting and integrating their inputs. Being a good collaborator and team player, even while leader of the team, is essential. And as digital technology makes any form easy to draw and construct, architects need to rethink what architectural forms are appropriate and can agglomerate into a larger, harmonious whole. Neither biomorphic blobs nor slick, minimalist boxes, for instance, can create satisfactory streets and urban tissue. Perhaps the virtues of composition and creating variants on a few recognizable types might need broader reassessment. Yet for its participants, the greatest legacy of the Ghost experience is an earned feeling of empowerment—a familiarity with and loss of fear about construction and construction sites—and a realization that even the most extreme constraints are no impediment to fine architecture.

Ghost 8

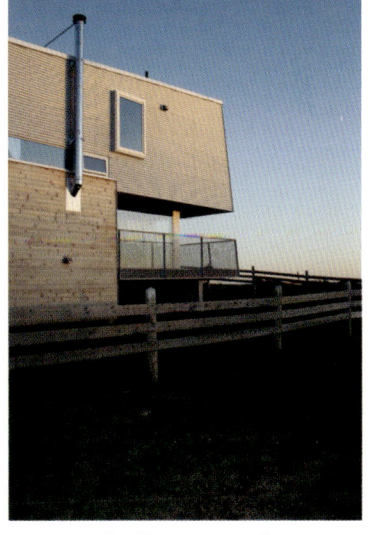

Corner   Studio sunset porch

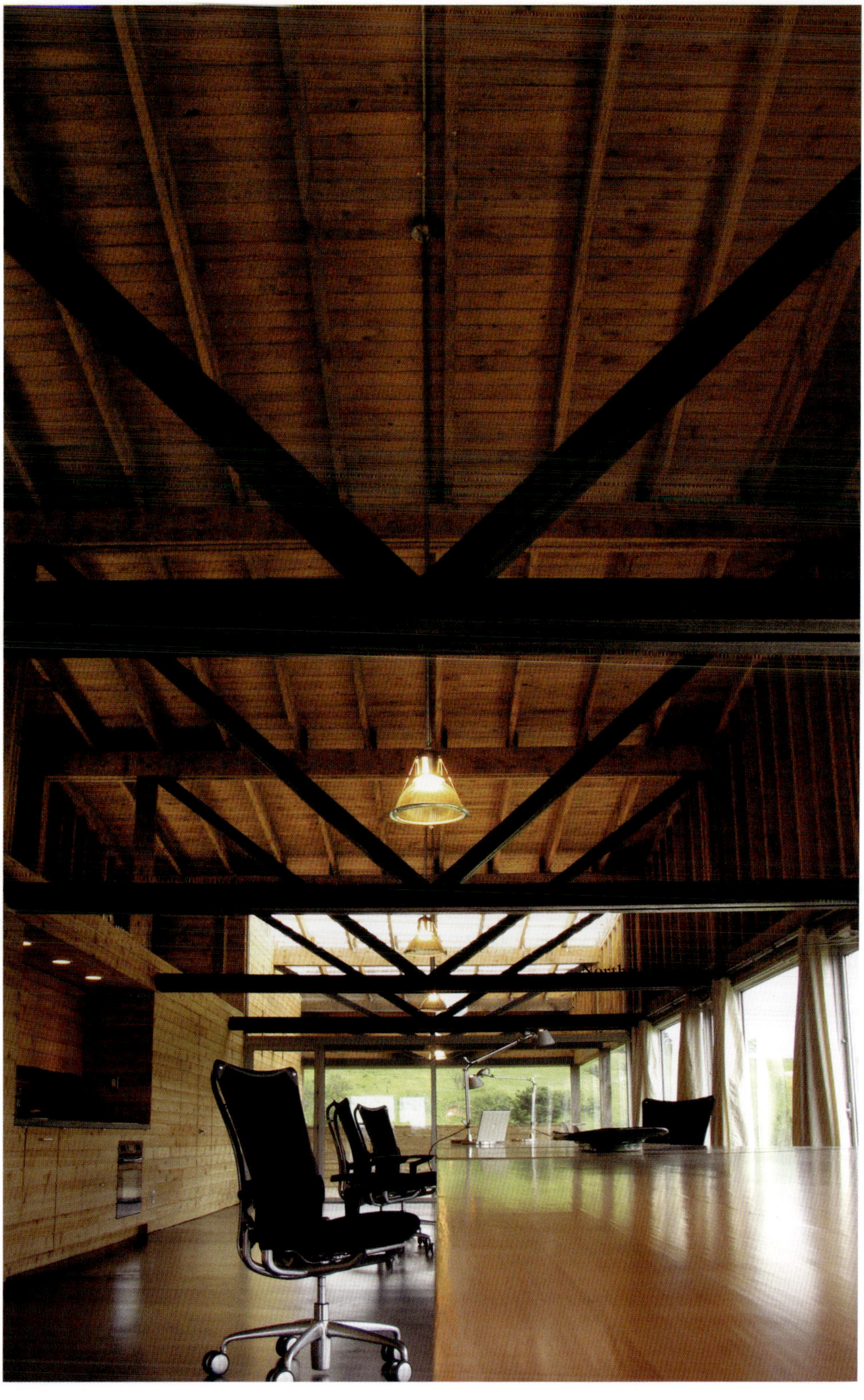

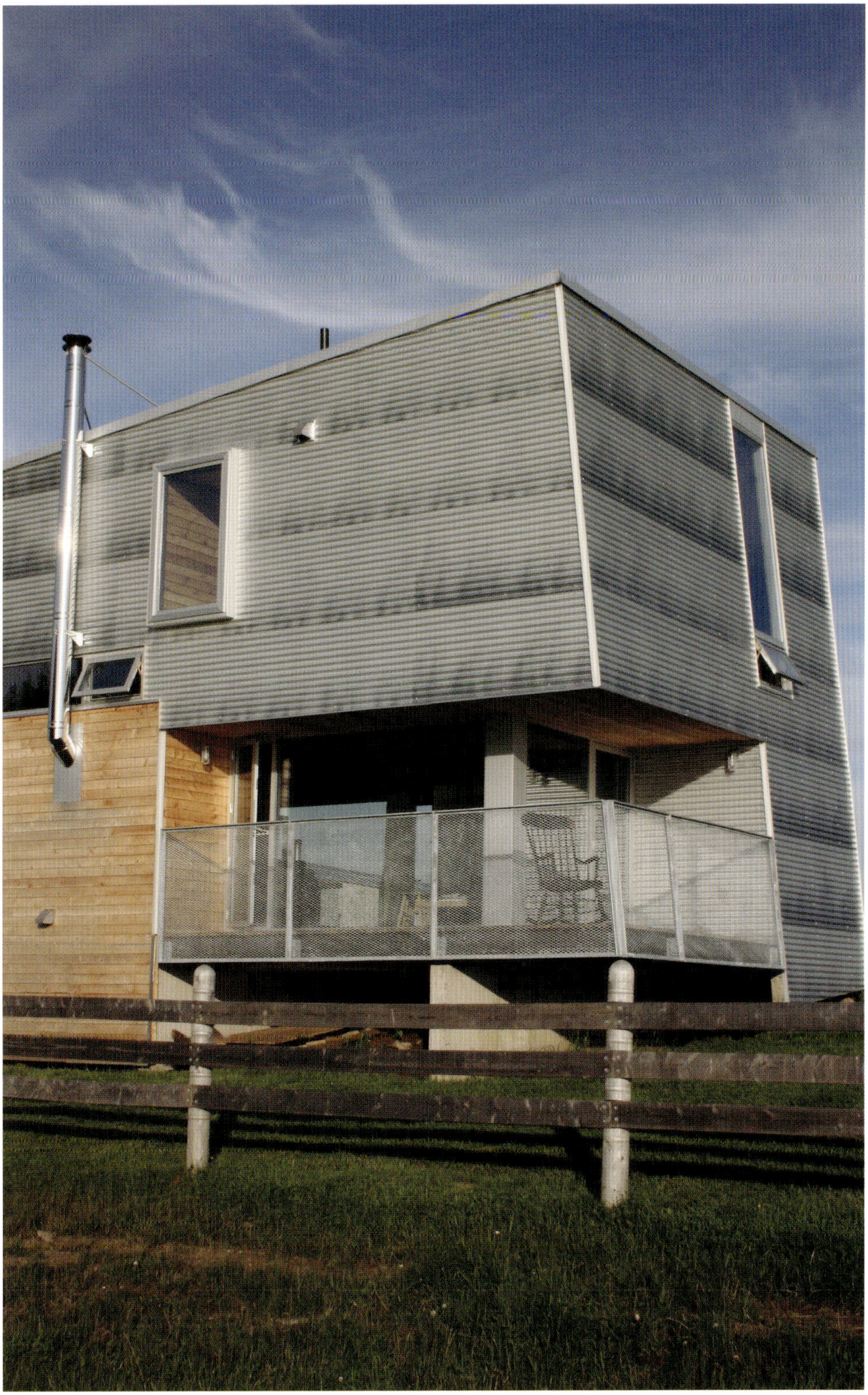

Hands to work, hearts to God

Willing

All architecture is a search for paradise on earth.
—Alvar Aalto

The human urge to build is a fundamentally optimistic act. Architects are in the business of optimism. We have no business with cynicism, pessimism, or dystopias. By the daily plying of our own trade, we can project a view of a better world. This has always been our job. It is both a lousy job and a privileged position, where we are constantly fighting against the default tendency toward mediocrity but with the possibility of occasionally redirecting this inertia into something exceptional.

According to urban historian Dolores Hayden, there are two utopian architectural traditions: The first is that if you are not satisfied with the world as it is, you retreat from it and build a new Jerusalem in the desert. The second is based on having empathy for the existing world as you find it and trying to improve it despite its flaws. In other words, if you are not satisfied with the world as it is, then change it. The Ghost Lab and the work of our practice, MacKay-Lyons Sweetapple Architects, which wraps around it, belong to the second tradition and are based on having faith in the ethical nature of architecture. As Sir Kenneth Clarke wrote in his book *The Gothic Revival: An Essay in the History of Taste* (1928): "The history of civilization has little to do with the facts, it is driven by ideas." We share the utopian commitment of the pioneers of the modern movement; we believe that architecture can reinforce ideas of place, social agency, sustainability, humanism, urbanism, and democracy—both materially and by example.

Architecture is the art of what you can cause to happen—making architecture an act of will, in spite of the odds. This kind of optimism cannot be easily taught. Perhaps it has more to do with one's natural temperament, the way that one's brain is wired—a sort of optimism set point. However, we can all think of role models, both in the academy and the street, who are disciplined optimists. What I am certain of is that this most valuable human commodity can be beaten out of us—think of a cynical professor, or mind-numbing work assigned by a corporate employer, or an unsupportive spouse at the end of each work day. In the face of a less-than-perfect world, it is easy to lose one's optimism.

Architects can choose to play an active role when it comes to the program of a building. What do we do when the client's brief of spatial requirements and aspirations is incomplete? We must maintain a critical position vis-à-vis the stated program and introduce extra programmatic content. While recently designing a new campus for a distinguished art college, MacKay-Lyons Sweetapple Architects found that the provided program contained insufficient social space for informal interaction due to budget constraints. During the participatory design workshops,

I kept writing the word "gallery" along the public face of the users' plans. Before long, the client began talking about the gallery during the construction phase; the contractors in the job trailer took to calling this room the "loggia." We had willed it into existence. During the designing of a new Canadian embassy in Dhaka, Bangladesh, it became clear that a post-9/11 world defines an embassy as a high-security building type—closed—rather than a public one—open and publicly accessible. We introduced a central courtyard, which, when read in conjunction with the few spaces open to the public within the project, created the impression of an extensive public domain. We willed public architecture while respecting the security requirements of the client.

The relationship between MacKay-Lyons Sweetapple Architects' projects and the environment is a prime opportunity to assert utopian values. The addition of a building to a landscape is an opportunity to improve or cultivate rather than for consumption. Sometimes this landscape is rural, other times urban. To add infill townhouses to a decaying urban streetscape is to reassert the belief in urbanism, to mend and idealize the idea of the street. In some instances, this guerilla urban design activity has saved a whole neighborhood from the wrecking ball. In the countryside, every new dwelling can help to reinforce the found natural or agrarian order by reintroducing cultivation. New quadrangles in conjunction with existing buildings have been created on every campus where the firm has built. This has domesticated or urbanized suburban campuses.

The greatest opportunity to assert one's idealism may be through the very design and construction process itself. The

American humanist architect Charles Moore said to me at the end of his life: "The only absolute architectural truth that I have found is that participatory design always works." MacKay-Lyons Sweetapple Architects employs this democratic method of working toward powerful consensus-based schemes in all the firm's projects—with the building's users, with the builders, and within the office. It is foolish to do otherwise and cut oneself off from authentic sources of content.

The Ghost Lab is a modest, built-utopian thesis. The relative freedom that the lab offers from conventional programmatic constraints allows us to focus on the higher programmatic ideals of community and urbanity. The dense aggregation of Ghost structures creates an ideal village or campus while protecting and conserving the surrounding agricultural landscape. The collaborative nature of the design-build process involves various Ghost participants and colleagues. The Ghost Lab and the community that surrounds it assert the view that there is but one world and that there is but one design project—life itself—that connects the ideas of family, practice, teaching, and community. Ghost is an act of willing paradises.

A simple parable of three bricklayers echoes the search for optimism in the architectural profession—that it is less significant what one does than how one thinks about one's actions. Three bricklayers are sitting together on the same scaffold. When questioned about what he is doing, the first bricklayer replies, "I am making a living." When asked the same question, the second bricklayer answers, "I am making a wall." When the third bricklayer is asked what he is up to, he asserts, "I am building a cathedral."

Ghost 8

Typical fishing schooner on water in front of Ghost site

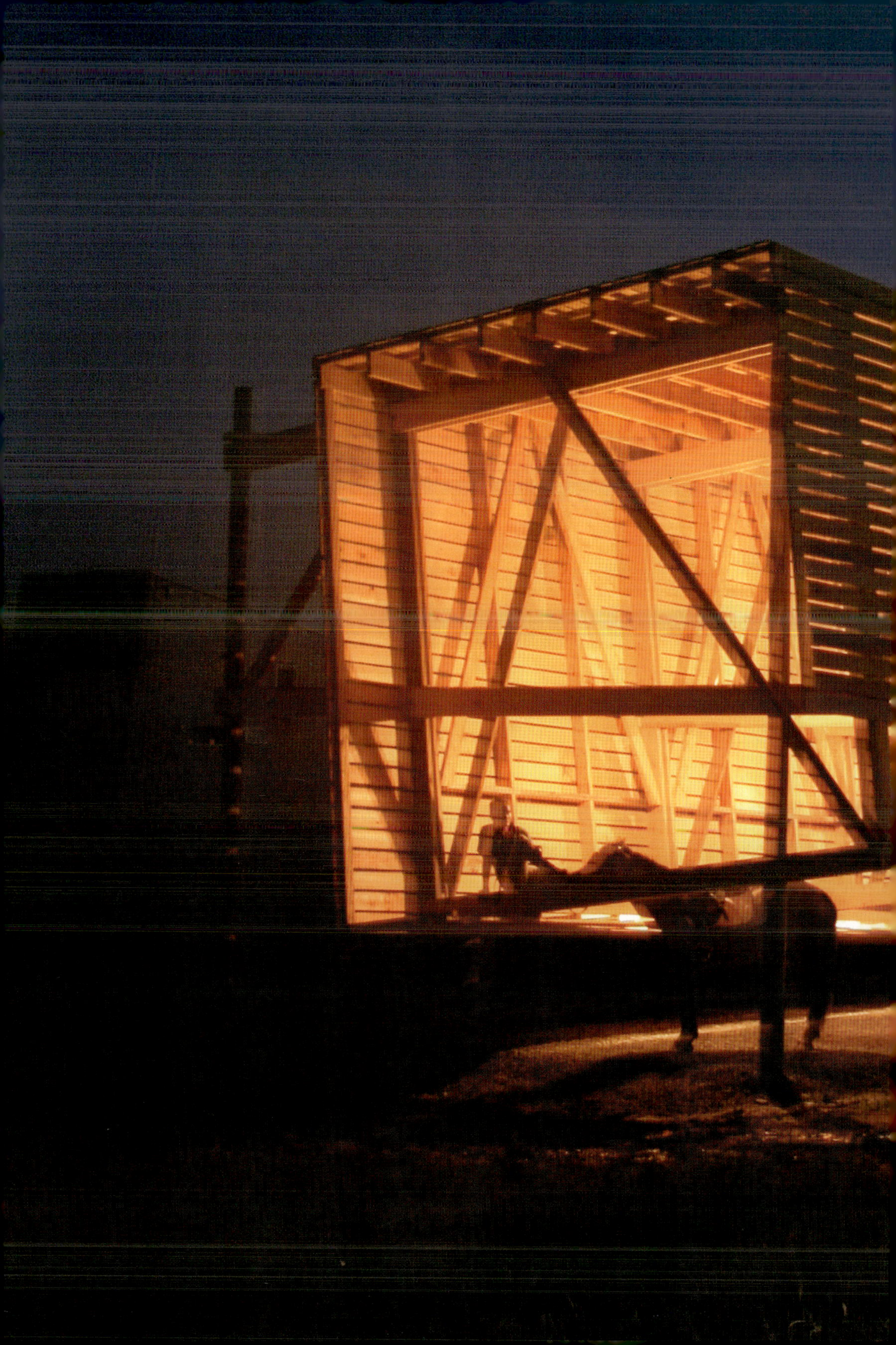

GHOST 9

June 30 to July 14, 2007

BLDG WITHIN BLDG

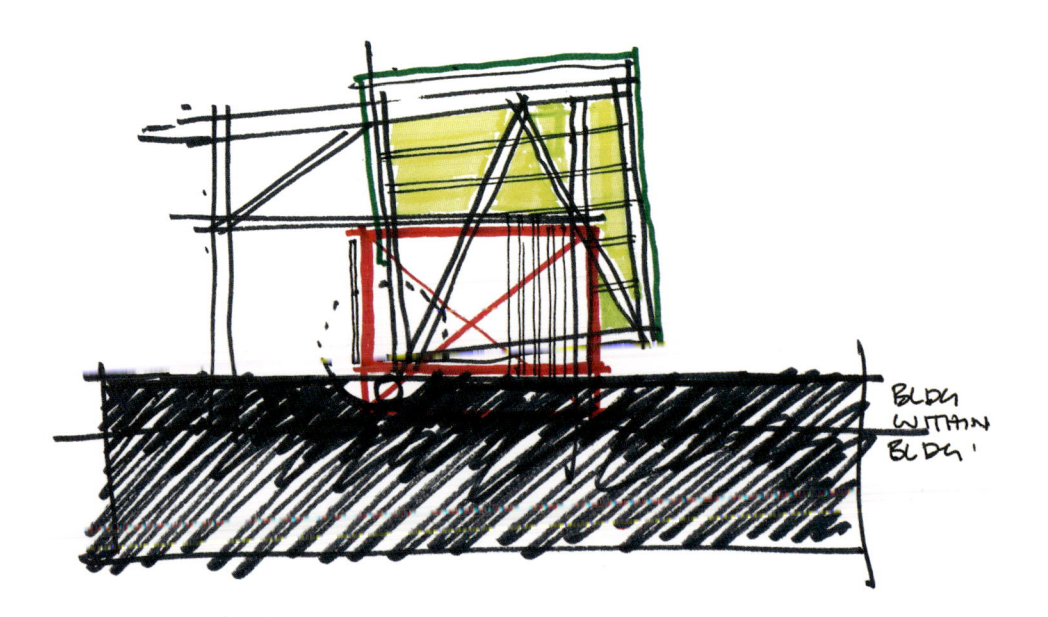

The Thought of Construction

Robert McCarter

In a valiant attempt to deal with the multiple personalities that seem required to be an architect today—practitioner, published form-maker, and professor—the Nova Scotian architect Brian MacKay-Lyons has, for a number of years, led a kind of triple life. First, he has, for some time now, been recognized as one of Canada's leading architects and has recently received steadily increasing attention in national and international publications. Second, he has, for a number of years, served as a professor of architecture at Dalhousie University (formerly the Technical University Nova Scotia until 1997) in Halifax. Third, over the last twenty-five years, in a critical regional practice *par excellence*, he has become what he calls the "village architect" for Kingsburg. In his village-architect practice, and in the closely associated Ghost Lab, MacKay-Lyons has found the means to bring together his three lives. As well as engaging participants from around the world, the annual two-week-long series of lessons-in-action rejoins thinking and making in architecture—lessons in what the Norwegian architect Sverre Fehn has called "the thought of construction."

The Ghost Lab, as well as all of MacKay-Lyons's work, is predicated on the belief that what really matters in architecture is not fashion and form but rather the tradition of building and the making of places. For MacKay-Lyons, architecture has everything to do with how its spaces are ordered to house the activities that take place within and between them; with how a building engages its place and the history of human occupation; with how a building is built, how it is structured, and of what materials it is made; and how all these affect what is experienced by those who inhabit it. In this, MacKay-Lyons is akin to the Finnish architect Alvar Aalto, who held that what matters is not what a building looks like the day it opens but what it is like to live in thirty years later.

Both thinking and making.
Such common-sense thinking is far removed, indeed, from what passes for academic discourse within many contemporary schools of architecture. Recently the dean of an influential Ivy League school of architecture informed his faculty that, today, academics can no longer be effective in both thinking and making, and, given the university's "definition" as a place of academic pursuits, the faculty should heretofore focus exclusively on thinking and no longer consider making in their teaching and research. It is appalling that such patently absurd and reductive "thinking," which seeks to define intellectual activities as those limited to thinking *without* making—as if such a thing were possible in architecture—is being voiced by leaders of schools where future generations of architects are now obligated, by law, to take their training.

In the 1960s, at the height of the dominance of architectural ideology based on a corporate definition of both clients and practices, the American architect Louis Kahn said, "The profession is in the marketplace; architecture is in the university." He believed that the profession, in his day, was no longer capable of engaging the essential aspects of architecture, which could only be discovered in the university. Today we must reverse this insight, for now the university is more and more in the (media) marketplace, whereas architecture lays in critical regional practices such as that of MacKay-Lyons Sweetapple Architects and in activities such as the Ghost Lab. Indeed, MacKay-Lyons first founded the Ghost project as a way of righting the imbalance he felt characterized architectural education, with its bias toward ungrounded and disengaged theorizing—thinking without making—and away from architectural practice, the experience of inhabitation, and the common sense engaged in all place-making. Thus the Ghost project was conceived as a means of binding together thinking and making, engaged and embodied in the action of building.

We only know what we make.
Upon his appointment as dean of the Venice School of Architecture and Urban Design in the 1960s, Carlo Scarpa had the aphoristic phrase of the eighteenth-century philosopher Giambattista Vico, *Verum ipsum factum* ("we only know what we make"), carved over the entry doors of the school and imprinted onto the diplomas. This ideal of thought embodied in construction precisely defines Scarpa's understanding of the training of an architect, and it may also serve as a motto for the Ghost Lab, where thinking and making, construing and constructing are joined irrevocably in enacting a work of architecture.

Today, we live in a time when many academics, having lost touch with their discipline, grasp irrelevant philosophical concepts and endeavor to impose them on the discipline—this despite the philosopher Karsten Harries's insight that "disciplines that are confident of their territory do not have much use for philosophy." The Ghost project allows the understanding that architecture has its own disciplinary tradition and ordering principles, unique unto itself, in its capacity to make place, to give identity, to construct community, and to shape experience—all through the understanding that we only know what we make.

Ghost 9

Modeling

Guest critic Robert McCarter

Deliberation

To retreat to advance.
With today's dominance of purely formal definitions of architecture and the placelessness characteristic of so-called globalized civilization, a danger is posed to both the discipline and the larger culture when leading architects take the position of the avant-garde, the advance guard, which moves forward through individual expressions into unknown territory (the future) by turning their backs on the history and principles of their discipline. The architectural historian Kenneth Frampton has argued, instead, for practitioners to assume the position of an arrière-garde, the rear guard, which turns and faces the past, protecting and conserving shared disciplinary principles. Here, it is also important to remember that the rear guard becomes the advance guard when a retreat is sounded.

    To retreat in order to advance is a primary premise for the Ghost Lab, predicated as it is on MacKay-Lyons staying in his remote place and the rest of the world, in the form of students and professionals, coming to him. The experience is dominated by the sense of retreat, the remoteness of the place, the presence of the changeable weather—warm sun one day and cold rain and thick fog the next—and the infinite ocean, its horizon the one true level. In this aspect of retreating to a remote place in order to return, as Kahn said, to the beginnings of one's discipline, the Ghost projects are an important model for relearning our craft, especially given our increasingly globalized condition. The remoteness of this place of retreat is paradoxically confirmed by the fact that the act of constructing the Ghost, a monastic undertaking par excellence, often takes place beneath a sky laced with the contrails of jets going to and from America to Europe at an altitude of five miles above the earth's surface.

The tradition of practice.
A great gulf separates our time from the time when Frank Lloyd Wright began his career by apprenticing in the office of Adler and Sullivan rather than attending the university, learning through making in what I have called "the tradition of practice." This tradition is a fully integrated experience binding all principles of the ethical practice of architecture—the economical, functional, ecological, constructive, structural, material, aesthetic, sensorial, social, and cultural aspects that together affect our experience of inhabitation, which remains the ultimate measure of a work of architecture. The results were buildings where every element has both a poetic and a practical character—the first of which was the architect's claim to success, the second taken entirely for granted as the minimal competence required to call oneself an architect.

The situation could not be more different today. We now take for granted the notion that architects specialize in providing very narrowly defined products—energy-efficient buildings, or ecologically sustainable buildings, or socially relevant buildings, or contextually appropriate buildings, or buildings of one functional type, or even buildings guaranteed to be published—but never all together, as in the tradition of practice. At the same time, by proffering their services anywhere around the globe and in the virtual world of the internet, the profession has abandoned its responsibilities to local culture, identity, and place.

The work of the Ghost Lab engages the tradition of practice, bound intimately as it always is to the local building culture and offering a far more integrated interpretation of sustainability. To be truly sustainable, a building must be accepted and used in its place and time, its social and cultural contexts, while always endeavoring, as Aalto said, to construct a paradise on earth.

Implicit in the Ghost project is the understanding that the separation—as specialized areas of expertise—of ecological sustainability, social relevance, energy efficiency, economy, historic preservation, landscape, urban design, among so many others, from mainstream architectural design—currently the norm in both education and practice is as destructive of disciplinary integrity as separating thinking from making, form from structure, space from use, or proportions from materials. In this the Ghost project suggests that the statement Wright made fifty years ago remains relevant: what we need most today is integrity in our architecture, which requires integrity in our social and cultural relations, integrity in our relationship to the land and environment, and integrity in our lives as inhabitants of architecture.

Liberative regionalism.
Harwell Hamilton Harris, architect and dean of the architecture school at the University of Texas, Austin, drew a distinction between two types of regionalisms in architecture in 1954. A *restrictive regionalism* is one that is defined by specific style and fixed forms and which is therefore closed and incapable of either adapting to changing situations or engaging universal civilization. A *liberative regionalism*, on the other hand, is defined by a set of ordering principles, which are grounded in its local culture, rather than any particular forms or style, and which is thereby open and capable of adapting itself to changing situations and, more importantly, appropriately engaging universal civilization in local culture. The terms *universal civilization* and *local culture* were coined by the French philosopher Paul Ricoeur, who also held that while civilization is available around the world (today's globalized condition), there is no culture that is not local, that does not belong to a particular place.

The Ghost projects exemplify this concept of liberative regionalism in that aspects of universal civilization are adapted to local culture, local ways of life, and to local materials and methods of making, reinventing and transforming both the universal and the local to make a unique and appropriate construction for its particular place and time. In this, we should not underestimate the importance of MacKay-Lyons's deep understanding—passed on each year to the Ghost participants—of the history of inhabitation, the characteristics of the climate and landform, the traditional methods of building and the nature of the materials at hand, and the myriad other interrelated aspects of the local culture in which he lives and works.

Studies in tectonic culture.
A critically important part of the Ghost Lab are the field trips to local buildings, both historical and contemporary, which include barns and farm complexes, fishing shacks set upon small rock islands, boat-building structures, vernacular houses, and works of MacKay-Lyons Sweetapple Architects. These lessons, among the most important of those imparted during the Ghost Lab, are studies in tectonic culture, primarily directed toward allowing the participants to gain an understanding of the local building tradition, and its adaptation in recent, modern constructions. This lesson is directly related to the dialectic of past and present about which the Mexican poet Octavio Paz writes: "If mutually isolated, tradition stagnates and modernity vaporizes; if joined, modernity breathes life into tradition and tradition responds by providing depth and gravity."

What is discovered here is a building tradition that deploys wood almost exclusively for both primary structure and enclosing skin, the rock foundations barely peeking above the surface

Ghost 9

One-to-one model

of the earth beneath the building. Examples include the elegant and articulate curved, weblike trusses of the boat-building structure, with its floor carved so as to allow the tide to enter and lift the completed boat; the small fishing shacks perched precariously on the rocks, more a part of the ocean than the land; the farm buildings that cluster around and form loosely defined, informal courtlike spaces between them; and the subtly angled boxlike volumes clad in wood and metal that typify MacKay-Lyons's own designs, with their carefully oriented walls of glass framing views of the village, landscape, and ocean. The common characteristics shared by these buildings are a sense of restraint and economy, of getting the greatest benefit from the least expenditure of material, energy, and space, and of an understated-yet-precise revelation of both the nature of local building materials and the age of the structures through the weathering they have undergone.

Listening to the land.
In the Ghost Lab site, MacKay-Lyons was able to spend innumerable hours walking, listening to the land—to the stories it tells of its previous inhabitation—before deciding the ideal place to build a house. In this search for the perfect balance of solar orientation, microclimate, topography, and view, he is much closer to the original settlers, who came and cleared the land that worked best for farming, than to the placeless and purely instrumental thinking ruling contemporary suburban housing developments. Property lines (the holy grail of land speculators) are meaningless here, and a local tradition of building, with its ecological-agricultural common sense, prevails.

After all, there is nothing more sustainable than a single-family farm, where one lives close to the bone, with no room for mistakes, relying on hard-won knowledge of climate, landscape, and vegetation (today called ecology) handed down from previous generations, who, quite literally, lived off the land. For MacKay-Lyons, the ruthless economy of vernacular farm buildings, with their precarious ecological balance, their severely limited resources, and their incremental adaptation of local materials to local climate and topography, serves as the appropriate measure for contemporary architecture built in this place. His example indicates that architects best serve their local culture by employing practices that leave the place in which they work more cultivated—capable of sustaining richer experiences of inhabitation—than when they first came to it.

Building the site.
While the Ghost projects seem to have an inevitable sense of belonging exactly to the place where they are sited, MacKay-Lyons has paradoxically stated that he usually visits a project site only once before construction starts. After this initial visit, he considers the site from a distance in plan and section, seeing what might be, how the perfection of this place, as paradise, can be willed into existence. Yet, building paradise on earth (Aalto's definition of architecture) cannot happen without a transformation of what was there before. Architecture and human inhabitation inevitably and irrevocably changes the context—be it urban or rural—and MacKay-Lyons does not shy away from this fact. As the Portuguese architect Alvaro Siza rightly observes, "architects do not invent anything; they transform reality."

For MacKay-Lyons, the construction and destruction that emerges from this process of making place often begins with the clearing of third-growth trees in order to reestablish the former agricultural fields and the ocean views they allowed. By cutting down and burning these trees—a ruthless process MacKay-Lyons

Ghost 9

Colleagues

Team photo

Guest architect Ted Flato

has often achieved largely by his own hand—he is returning the land closer to an earlier condition of human inhabitation, one characterized by the ecological balance typical of farm economies, which "touch this earth lightly," as the Australian architect Glenn Murcutt advocates.

MacKay-Lyons is also close to the Swiss architect Luigi Snozzi, who, not coincidentally, has for thirty years served as "village architect" for Monte Carasso and his protégé, Mario Botta, when they speak of "building the site." Building the site, as a cultivation of the land, whether rural or urban, involves looking both forward and backward, using the traces of the history of agricultural or architectural inhabitation of the site—a true form of culture always unique in its response to the local climate and building traditions—to counteract the current ravages of suburban sprawl and overdevelopment, inevitably the same around the world.

Setting the bounds for the space within.
The collection of buildings that make up Ghost, both individually and collectively, are fundamentally concerned with making boundaries, edges that frame and form the space of inhabitation. Often variations on the vernacular agricultural complexes' south-facing courtyards and great rooms, these spaces are in experience a merging of interior and exterior. Each interior room is first bounded and defined, then opened to the landscape—two of its four sides are solid, often thickened with service elements, while the other two sides are open, framing the space defined by an L-shaped plan. The occupied diagonal, as a room or as a courtyard formed between two buildings, opens out to the landscape beyond. In this way, MacKay-Lyons is able to draw the landscape, the village, the ocean, and even the distant horizon into the experience of the inhabitants.

As Wright noted, the primary purpose of architecture is to construct a bounded place, a sheltered interior, which serves not as the object of our attention but as a background or framework for the daily life that takes place within it. This remarkably modest definition of the task of architecture suits MacKay-Lyons equally well. Another parallel between his architecture and that of Wright is their evolution of building types as variations on a theme. MacKay-Lyons Sweetapple Architects' buildings evoke Wright's midcentury Usonian Houses: their simple rectangular geometries, L-shaped plans, two closed (thickened service walls) and two open sides framing their south-facing courtyards, typical construction of horizontal wood-board siding, solid concrete floors with embedded radiant heat, subtle and understated detailing, unmatched experiential qualities of light and space, and seamless integration with their natural place.

Limitations are the architect's best friends.
One of the characteristics of the Ghost Lab—as well as all great works of architecture—is the severity of the limitations within which the makers are required to operate. In the case of the Ghost project, the limitations are of both material and time, as the structure must be designed and built within only two weeks, using locally milled wood. This goes directly against what is typical of most contemporary architecture, which prides itself on an appearance of being born without limitations, and against what occurs in many schools, where issues of economy are ignored. This approach avoids the realities of a world of ever-decreasing resources and the fundamental responsibility of the architect to act in the best interests of the community. There is a misguided understanding that accepting limitations will somehow curtail the freedom of expression of the student, and that excessive budgets have often led to so-called inventions in architecture.

Igor Stravinsky, the Russian composer, writes: "Only within strict limitations is freedom possible," pointing out the fundamental truth that without limitations, there can be no freedom. Pertinent to this so-called freedom that comes without limits, and the results we see around us in the form of architecture as a form of self-expression, is Wright's stinging observation that "the sins of architects are permanent sins." Wright also notes that, both in his own practice of architecture and in the history of architecture that he studied, he had come to the conclusion that "limitations are the architect's best friends"—a phrase that could well serve as a motto for the Ghost Lab.

Monumentality and handcraft.
This year's Ghost project, a horse barn, is at once abstract and geometric, characterized by an ephemeral monumentality, and also every inch a handmade thing. Insight into this dichotomous condition, and its relation to the history of modern architectural pedagogy, is found in Kahn's and the German artist Josef Albers's essays read at a 1944 symposium. Kahn's essay defines monumentality as, paradoxically, independent of scale or expense, with an eternal, spiritual quality imparted by the manner in which a building is constructed. "Neither the finest material nor the most advanced technology need enter a work of monumental character," Kahn states, for the same reason that the quality of the Magna Carta had nothing to do with the cost of the ink—in architectural terms, it had to do with the work, the thought, the craft, the "striving for structural perfection" that went into its making. Albers, in an essay titled—significantly enough in this context—"The Educational Value of Manual Work and Handicraft in Relation to Architecture," argues that architects, whose process of design involves making drawings for others (builders) to use in the actual construction, must be educated learning to experience

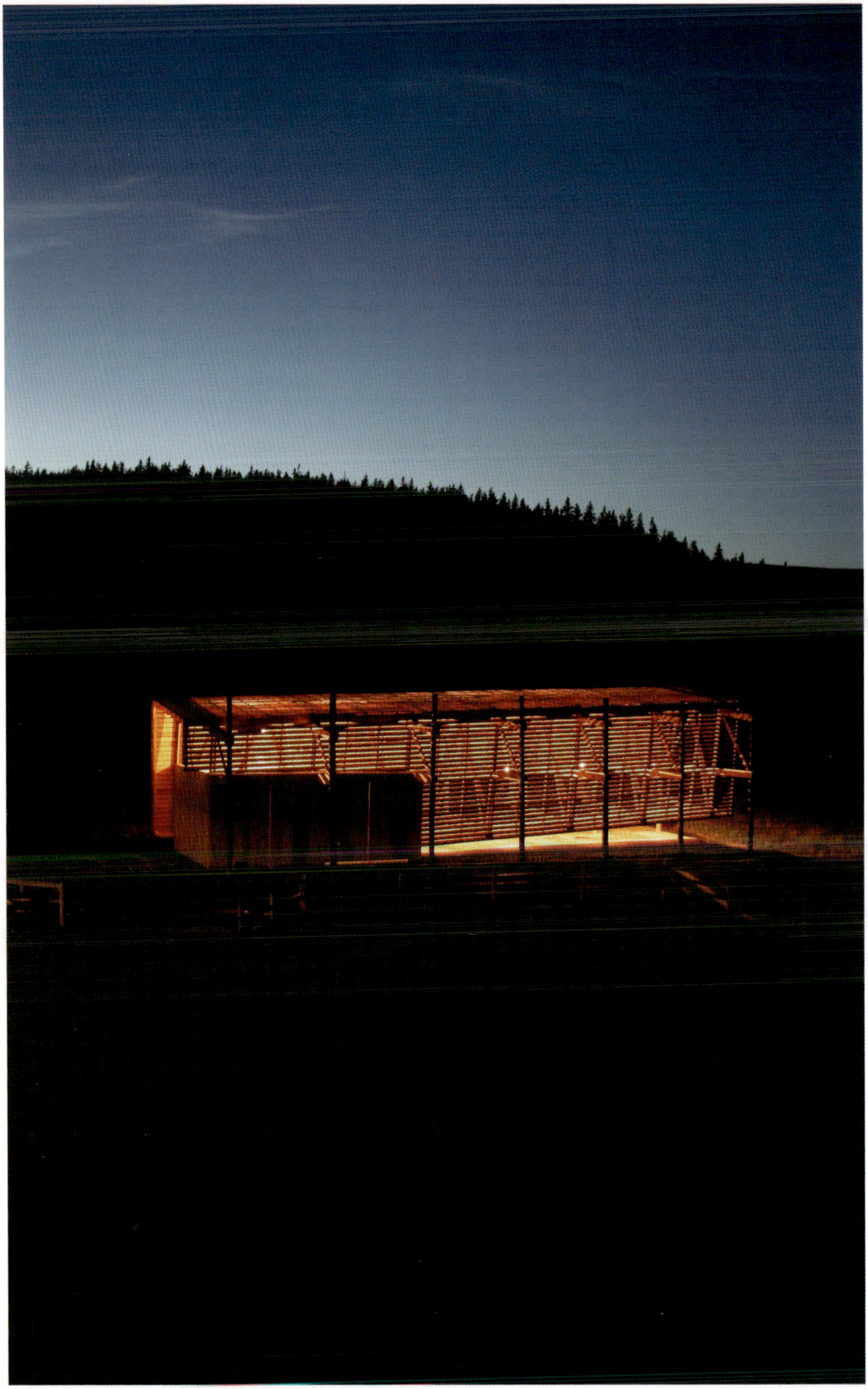

the qualities of the materials with which they build and to reveal in the finished building the process of its construction.

The dictation of materials.
During the second week of Ghost—well into the construction of the barn, whose design was only tangentially related to any barn precedents and was much more closely related to certain geometric notions of rotating squares derived from modern art—the group decided to realign the structure's preexisting columns, pulling several of them out of true in order to allow uniform-sized framing members for the whole and to minimize cutting. This realignment was a requirement of construction, not form, and it seemed at the time a significant moment in the process, a kind of pivot between pure geometry as determinant and the thought of construction as determinant.

Far too few projects today ever undergo such a critically important transition in thinking. In much contemporary architecture, the form is all that matters, and it remains largely unchanged by the process of being built. Today architects both design and compose construction documents in the virtual space of the computer, leaving the entire process literally untouched by human hands. In the Ghost project, on the other hand, the initial geometric form, pure in a certain way, is transformed by four questions: first, how to *imagine* building it at all, especially given the structural engineer's initial skepticism toward the design; second, how it *should* be built, that is, how to build it in a way appropriate to the material (local hemlock and spruce), to work, as Wright said, in the nature of the materials; third, how it *could* be built, given the group's widely varying levels of construction experience; and fourth, how it *was* built, that is, how, in the act of building, the purity of the form was modified by requirements of suitability to function and clarity of construction. In the end, form, function, and construction were balanced through a series of decisions that had to do with appropriateness. In this it is intriguing to recall that Kahn once said, "All I teach in the university is appropriateness."

Many of the most important lessons of Ghost are learned by touch and hearing, through the hand and the body feeling the wood's weight, grain, and hardness, through the sound of a nail driven in true. Both design and construction decisions are made based upon the local climate's effects on various building materials. Once completed and put into use, the building is largely characterized by what Kahn called "the marks of making," such as the nail patterns that reveal the underlying structure. All these materially determined aspects of the project's conception and construction may be directly related to a 1946 statement by the weaver Anni Albers: "Being creative is perhaps not the desire to do something, but listening to that which wants to be done, the dictation of the materials."

The construction of experience.
One of the strengths of the Ghost Lab is its numerous layered and overlapping agendas, among which are the correction of the bias toward thinking without making in architectural education; the evolution of a contemporary merger of the universal and local, the vernacular and modern; the reengagement of the body in making and inhabiting; the reintegration of architecture and agriculture as two related ways of cultivating the land; reestablishing the importance of place—with its climate, landform, geology, sunlight, and its history of inhabitation, cultivation, and construction—in the making of architecture; and, most importantly, the integration of the *thought of construction* through the *construction of experience,* realized in the group's shared act of

designing and building. "Ethics and aesthetics are one in the same," stated the Austrian philosopher Ludwig Wittgenstein.

Part of the real success of the Ghost Lab is the understanding that, in the end, architecture lies in the realm of experience and the act of making, not in the academy or in corporate practice where words dictate results. As the American philosopher Ralph Waldo Emerson notes: "No answer in words can reply to a question of things." The Ghost project has most to do with things that can only be made and learned by being there, indicating that if we are to learn anything of fundamental importance about the discipline of architecture, we must experience it in the flesh as constructive lessons in thinking and making, inextricably bound together in the thought of construction.

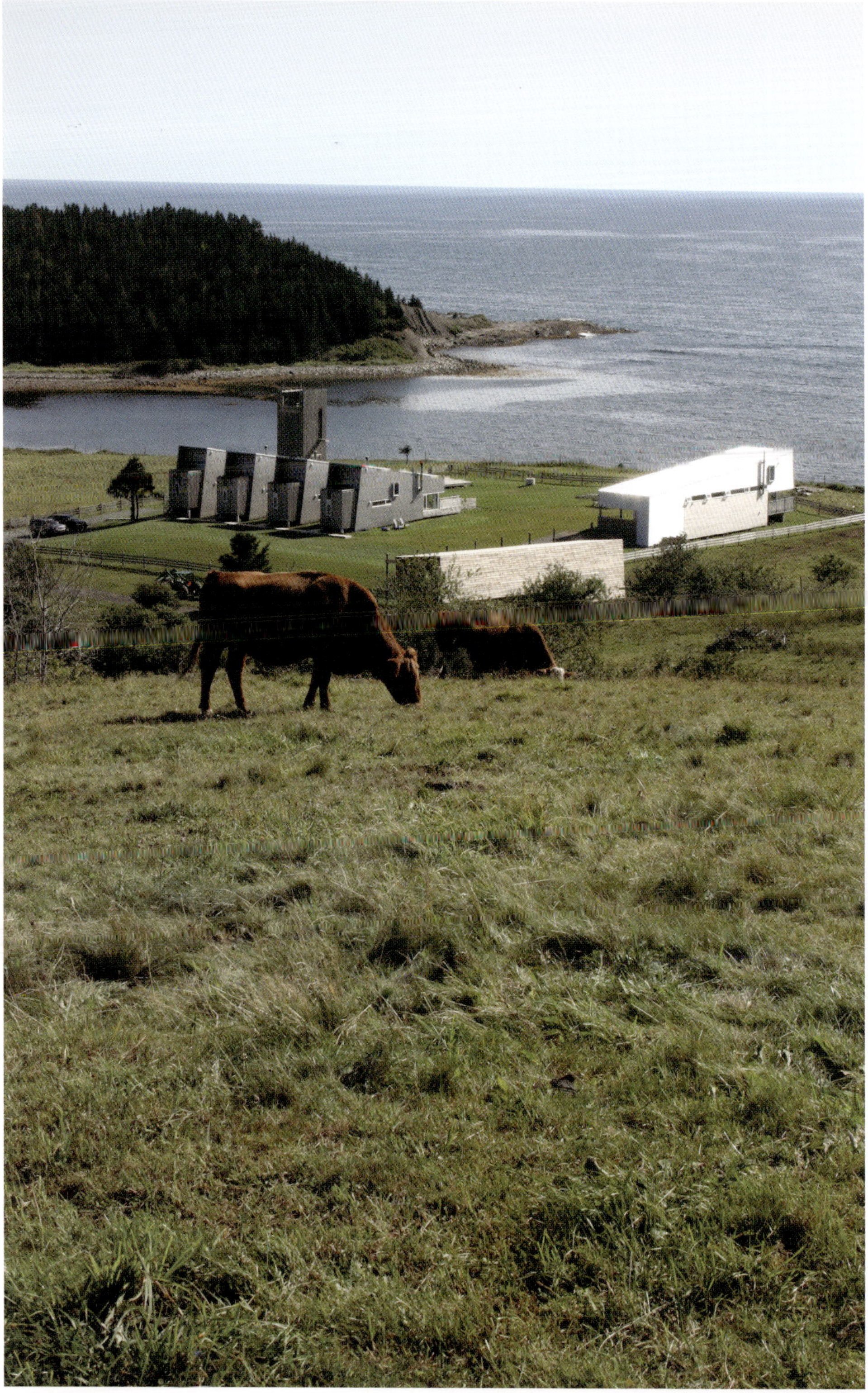

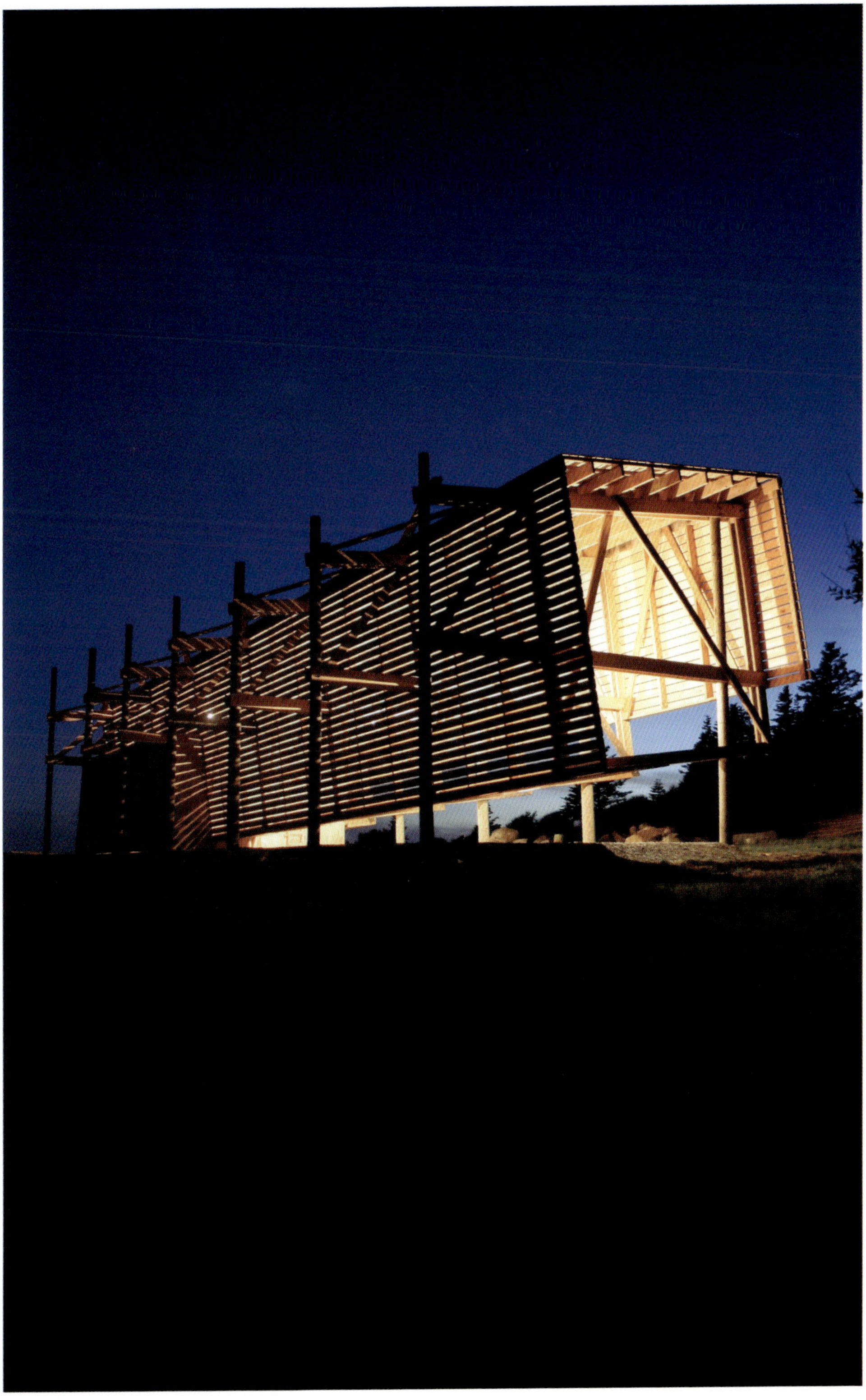

Kingsburg

Listening

> *The hallucinatory effect derives from the extraordinary clarity and not from mystery or mist. Nothing is more fantastic ultimately than precision.*
> —Alain Robbe-Grillet on Franz Kafka's *Metamorphosis*

After a recent lecture in San Francisco, an architect asked, "Where do you want to be in ten years? What kind of work do you want to be doing?" I responded that I wanted to make buildings that are more invisible, yet more didactic; buildings that are more silent, yet speak more clearly.

Good conversation requires both listening and speaking. In responsive architectural design, there is often little difference between the questions being asked and the proposition being made. The Italian architect Giancarlo de Carlo asserted that the quality of one's design proposition is directly tied to the depth of one's reading of the context. John Berger's *Ways of Seeing: Based on the BBC Television Series* (Penguin, 1990) has taught a generation of visual artists the discipline of visual listening. Norwegian architectural historian Christian Norberg Schulz's book *Genius Loci* (Rizzoli, 1991) is a thesis about place-informed architecture. For American architect Charles Moore, listening was an essential component in the process of the making of a democratic architecture. Louis Kahn said, "I neither read nor write, I observe." Designing is a method for studying one's world.

Through the work of MacKay-Lyons Sweetapple Architects and through the Ghost Lab, I have conducted a long conversation with the Ghost site, based on an earnest desire to communicate rather than to mystify. It is both a conversation about specificity of place and ideas that are universal, about a particular time and timelessness. Many of the firm's projects can be seen as devices for viewing the landscape or surveying instruments. They exploit natural conditions, like the geomorphology of the site and its attendant flora and fauna; they listen to the syncopated rhythms of the sea. They are essays on climate and weathering, responding to the effects of sun and wind. They are studies in cultural processes of human settlement on the land. They are didactic lessons about the processes of their making and their underlying material culture. They express themselves as the result of a sequence of trades coming to and going from the site or as embodied labor. Each element, structural member, or nail must declare its role in making the whole ensemble or be edited out of the conversation. Speak clearly or not at all.

The various Ghost projects listen and speak to found conditions, the conditions of making, and, by aggregation, they speak with each other. They articulate the spaces that are made between them. These interstitial places are analogous to the use of white space in painting, the public space system in Nolli's famous map of Rome, or the silent pauses in music. They are, at once, the most invisible and most charged aspect of our architecture. They are simultaneously void and solid.

During the design process for Ghost 9, a participant asked, "Which single element on the site should the project relate to?" I replied that it must resonate with all elements of the site simultaneously—side hill, back hill, studio, cabin roofs, tower, cabin bed boxes, fence—not just one and that this should be done with the simplest form and the minimum means. In his *The Ten Books on Architecture*, the Roman architectural theorist Vitruvius argued that the two most important measures of architecture were *claritas* (clarity) and *symmetria* (the commensurability of the parts). These criteria have continued to be common to all areas of creative human endeavor, in the arts and in the sciences. The concept of elegance is eternal—do the most with the least.

As a child I became an oral learner rather than a book learner due to a learning disability. I learned by listening, by asking questions of my elders. It is a charmed existence—after all, it is human nature to enjoy being asked for one's opinion and being respected as a community storyteller. Therefore, as the listener, I have been treated generously by my elders. So now I, too, have become a storyteller through the lens of the discipline of architecture. I am not a writer but a Saturday-afternoon companion, walking through the landscape among past and future ghosts.

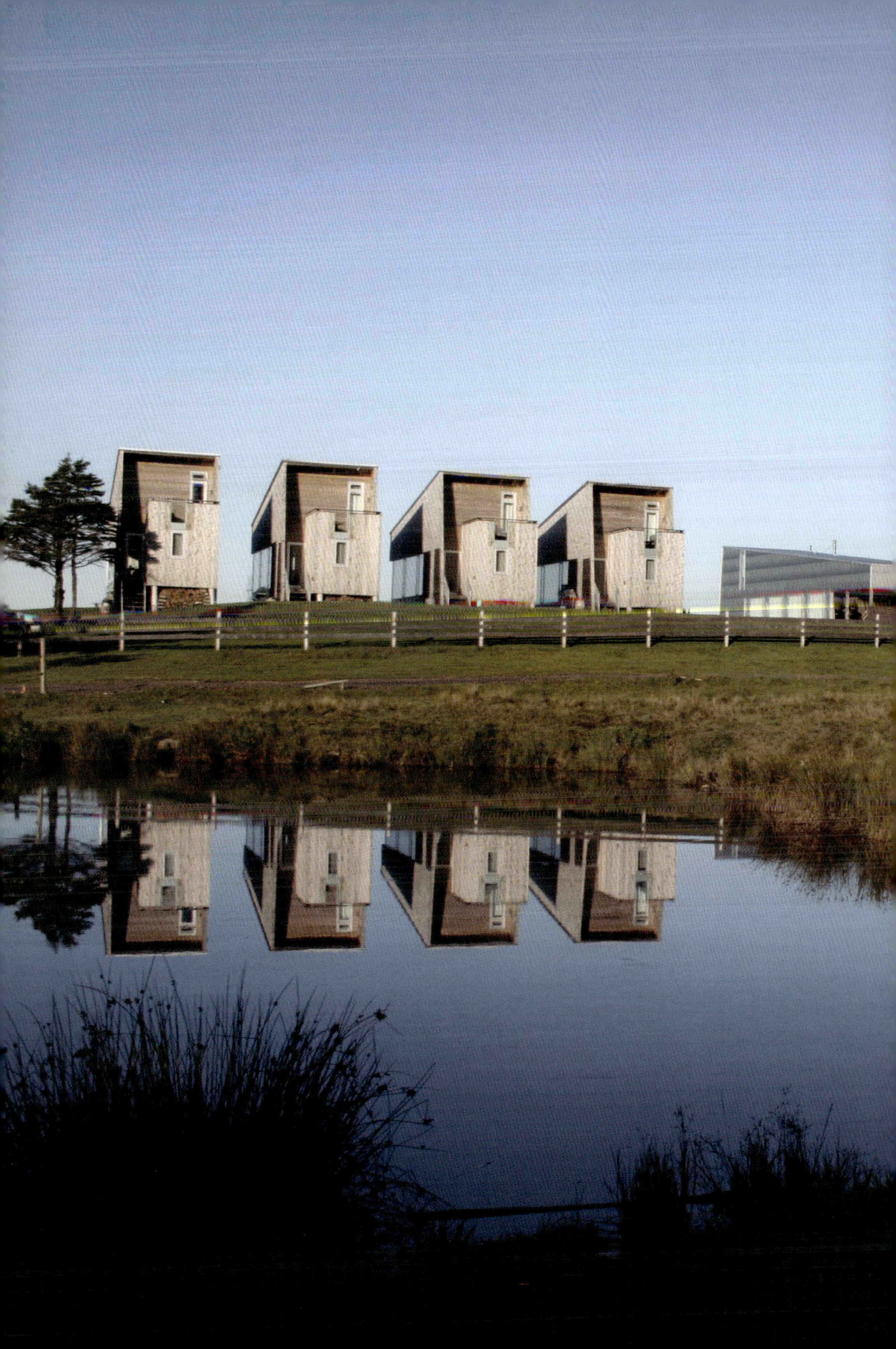

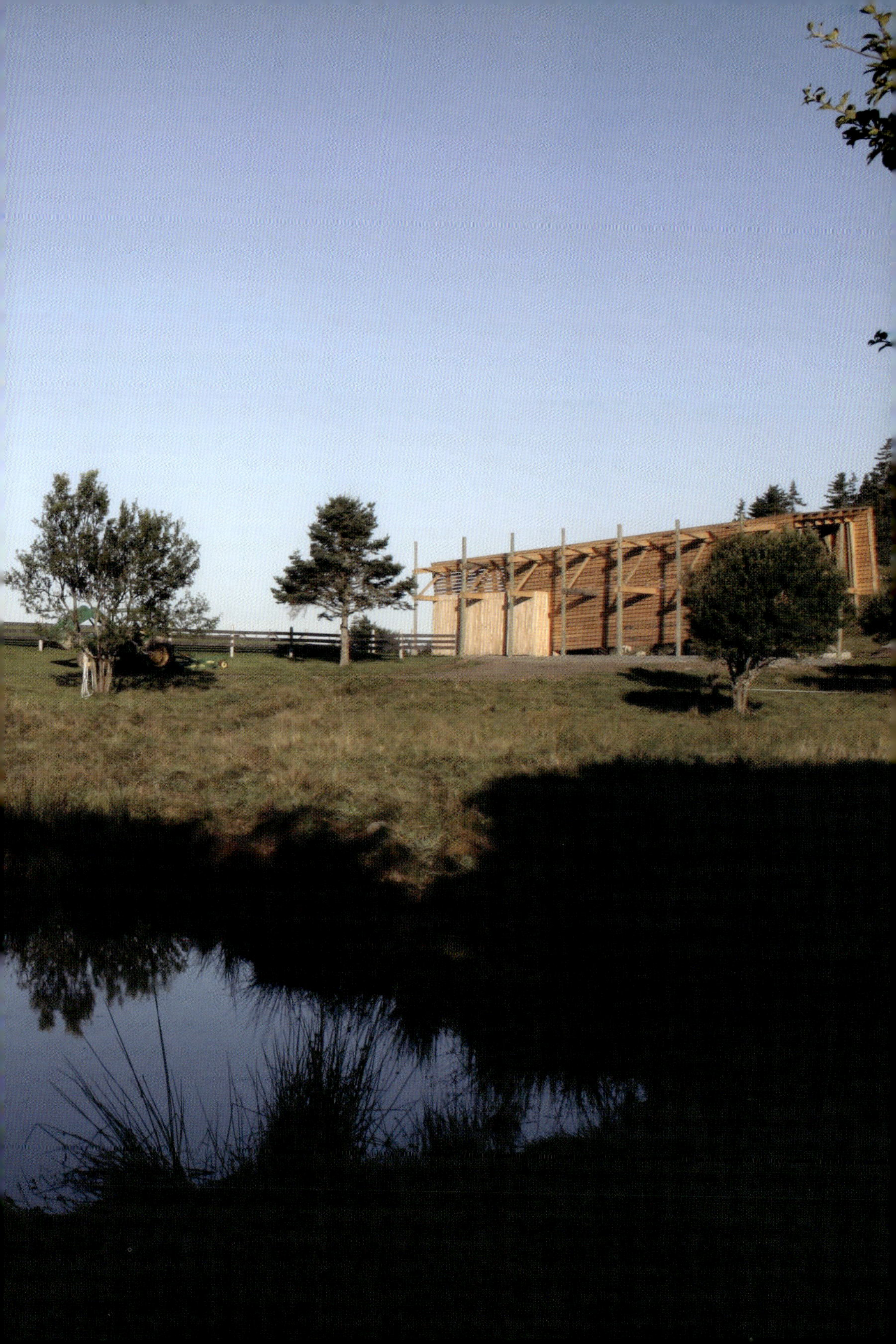

Contributor Biographies

A writer, critic, consultant, and curator, **Peter Buchanan** worked as an architect and urban designer/planner before joining *Architect's Journal* and *Architectural Review* in 1979, becoming deputy editor of the latter in 1982. He began freelancing in 1992 and has since curated traveling exhibitions. His books include the four volumes of *Renzo Piano Building Workshop: Complete Works* (Phaidon Press, 1999) and *Ten Shades of Green* (W.W. Norton, 2005).

Brian Carter is an architect and the designer of a number of award-winning buildings. He was appointed chair of architecture at the University of Michigan in 1994. The author of several books, including *Johnson Wax Administration Building and Research Tower* (Phaidon Press, 1998), his writings on architecture and design have also appeared in numerous international professional journals. Carter was appointed professor and dean of the School of Architecture and Planning at the State University of New York at Buffalo in 2002.

Thomas Fisher is a professor of architecture and dean of the College of Design at the University of Minnesota. He is currently a contributing editor at *Architecture Magazine*. His recently published books include *In the Scheme of Things: Alternative Thinking on the Practice of Architecture* (University of Minnesota Press, 2000) and *Salmela Architect* (University of Minnesota Press, 2005) and *Lake/Flato: Buildings and Landscapes* (Rockport Press, 2005).

Kenneth Frampton practiced as an architect for a number of years in the United Kingdom and in Israel and served as the editor of the British magazine *Architectural Design*. He has taught at Princeton University and the Royal College of Art, London. He currently holds the position of the Ware Professor of Architecture at Columbia University. His publications include *Modern Architecture: A Critical History* (Thames & Hudson, 1980), *Studies in Tectonic Culture* (MIT Press, 1995), *Le Corbusier* (HNA Books, 2001), and *Labour, Work and Architecture* (Phaidon Press, 2002).

Karl Habermann served as editor in chief of the specialist architectural review *Detail* from 1990 to 1998. Since then Habermann has worked as an independent architect and expert author in Munich. His publications include *Energy Efficient Architecture* (Birkhäuser Basel, 2006) and *Staircases: Spiral and Corkscrew* (Random House, 2006). His various work experiences include the preservation of historical monuments, design and building of hospitals, and various competitions.

Robert Ivy became editor in chief of *Architectural Record* in November 2006, a period of expansion for the 116-year-old magazine. At *Record* Ivy has encouraged recognition of regionally appropriate work ("Out There: Architecture Outside the Centers of Fashion," February 2001, featuring the work of Brian MacKay-Lyons). Formerly a principal in a successful architectural practice and a critic for national publications, his book on the late architect Fay Jones, *Fay Jones* (McGraw-Hill, 2001), remains the standard reference on the subject.

Christine Macy is a professor of architectural design and history at Dalhousie University in Canada. She established her partnership, Filum, in 1990, specializing in lightweight structures and public space design for festivals. Regional editor of *Canadian Architect*, her books include the coauthored *Architecture and Nature: Creating the American Landscape* (Routledge, 2003), which received the Alice Davis Hitchcock Award in 2005, and *Festival Architecture* (Routledge, 2007).

Robert McCarter is a practicing architect, professor, and author. The Ruth and Norman Moore Professor of Architecture at the Sam Fox School of Design and Visual Arts, Washington University in St. Louis, Missouri, McCarter has also taught at the University of Florida (director of the school of architecture from 1991 to 2001), Columbia University, the University of Louisville, and North Carolina State University. McCarter's publications include *Frank Lloyd Wright: Critical Lives* (Reaktion, 2006) and *Louis I. Kahn* (Phaidon, 2005).

Juhani Pallasmaa is active in urban planning, architecture, and exhibition, product, and graphic design. He has held many academic positions including professor and dean of Helsinki University of Technology and director of the Museum of Finnish Architecture. Pallasmaa has published numerous books and essays in thirty languages, including *Encounters: Architectural Essays* (Rakennustieto Publishing, 2005) and *The Eyes of the Skin: Architecture and the Senses* (John Wiley & Sons, 1995).

Ghost Participants

Ghost 1 (1994) / critic and all participants from Technical University of Nova Scotia (currently Dalhousie University)
Critic: Christine Macy
Matt Beattie, Nicole Delmage, Carolyn Jeffs, Glen MacMullin, Zane Murdoch, Jim Pfeffer, Sean Rodrigues, Talbot Sweetapple, Mike Woodland

Ghost 2 (1995) / all participants from Technical University of Nova Scotia (currently Dalhousie University)
Critic: Brian Carter, State University of New York, Buffalo
Chris Allen, Audrey Archambault, Trevor Davies, Stephanie Forsythe, Rod Gillis, Alistair Huber, Philip Jefferson, David Jensen, Collen Lashuk, Alison MacNeil, Chris Oxner, Michael Rudnicki, Jason Smirnis

Ghost 3 (1997) / all participants from Dalhousie University
Critic: Karl Habermann, editor, *Detail*
Mehira Ebdel Aziz, Ben Duffell, Mike Farrar, Nicola Grigg, Ron Isaac, Viktoria Mygoro, Richard Nowlan, Trevor Thimm, Krista Wuere

Ghost 4 (2002)
Architect: Bob Benz, Thomas Anderson & Co.
Critic: Robert Ivy, editor, *Architectural Record*
Josh Barandon, Massachusetts Institute of Technology
Tarrah Beebe, Catholic University of America
Scott Cryer, University of North Carolina at Charlotte
Vanessa Eng, University of Maryland
Rory Heath, Dalhousie University
Erika Klemm, Illinois Institute of Technology
John Lacy, Syracuse University
Stephanie Lam, Dalhousie University
Perry Poole, University of North Carolina at Charlotte
Vincent Van Den Brink, Dalhousie University
Terri Whitchead, Dalhousie University

Ghost 5 (2003)
Architect: Rick Joy, Rick Joy Architects
Critic: Kenneth Frampton, Columbia University
Jane Abbot, Dalhousie University
Nicholas Bourque, University of Louisiana at Lafayette
Andrew Corrigan, Rice University
Kelli David, Dalhousie University
John C. Fleming, University of Michigan
Jeff Gonsoulin, University of Louisiana at Lafayette
Nicholas Groch, University of North Carolina at Charlotte
Whitney Izor, Syracuse University

Chris Johns, Massachusetts Institute of Technology
Etinne Lemay, Dalhousie University
William Martella, University of Tennessee
Justin Park, Texas Tech University
Martin Patriquin, Dalhousie University
Paul Pierson, Cornell University
Russell Rudzinski, University of Arkansas
Jeff Schroeder, Frank Harmon Architects
Mohamed Sheriff, Illinois Institute of Technology
Lauren Wise, University of North Carolina at Charlotte

Ghost 6 (2004)
Architect: Wendell Burnett, Arizona State University
Critic: Thomas Fisher, College of Design, University of Minnesota
Bryan Anderson, Sala Architects Inc.
Laura Baker, Mississippi State University
Kate Busby, Dalhousie University
Frank Flury, Illinois Institute of Technology
Tina Grieger, New York, NY
Bryce Hamels, Texas Tech University
Charles Howell, University of North Carolina
Dawn Lang, Dalhousie University
Nuria Montblach, Dalhousie University
Annie Pelletier, Dalhousie University
Sara Queen, Frank Harmon Architects
Robin Ramcharan, Syracuse University
Jesse Ratcliffe, Dalhousie University
Chuck Rotolo, Washington University in St. Louis
Marcin Sztaba, Dalhousie University
Myles Trudell, University of Tennessee

Ghost 7 (2005)
Architect: Marlon Blackwell, Marlon Blackwell Architects; Rick Joy, Rick Joy Architects
Critic: Juhani Pallasmaa, Helsinki University of Technology
Jeffrey Barrett, California College of Arts
Felicity Bristow, Helen Lucas Architects
Laura Duris, University of Maryland
Gisèle Edwards, Arizona State University
Andy Emke, Washington University in St. Louis
Matthew Englehaupt, Sala Architects Inc.
Troy Gallas, University of Minnesota
Allison Gonsalves, Dalhousie University
Matthew Hall, Matthew Hall Design
Natalie Jones, University of North Carolina at Charlotte
Heath MacDonald, University of Texas at Arlington
Mara Marcu, University of Houston
Lorelei Martin, Texas Tech University
Tahar Messadi, University of Arkansas
Samuel Olshin, Atkin Olshin Lawson-Bell Architects
Kara Pegg, University of Arkansas
Stephen Robertson, National Capital Commission
Regin Schwaen, Virginia Tech University
Steve Southerland, The Miller/Hull Partnership
Amber Trimble, Carleton University
Richard Webre, Mississippi State University
Jaime Widows, Syracuse University
Paul Winter, University of North Carolina
Sally Wurtzler, Washington University in St. Louis

Ghost 8 (2006)
Architect: David Miller, The Miller/Hull Partnership; Bob Benz, Thomas Anderson & Co.
Critic: Peter Buchanan, London, United Kingdom
Renata Carettoni Abma, California Institute of the Arts
David Archer, University of Arkansas
John Blake, Miami University of Ohio
Sarah Calandro, Louisiana State University
Christian Callaghan, Syracuse University
Morgan Carter, Dalhousie University
Melissa Clark, University of Arkansas
Jason Cross, University of New Mexico
Victor Ebergenyl, Universidad Nacional Autonoma de Mexico
Nathaniel Felder, University of Washington
Carey Givens, Louisiana State University
Jerry Greer, Arizona State University
James Hill, Virginia Tech University
Bill Holloway, Mississippi State University
Jessica Erin Johnson, Texas Tech University
Mike Johnson, University of Manitoba
Kasey Josephs, University of Arizona
John Klebanowski, University of North Carolina at Charlotte
Lindsey MacDonald, Syracuse University
Brad Manning, University of Minnesota
Patrick Martin, University of Southern California
Zui Lig Ng, University of Houston
Bianca Pulitzer, Southern California Institute of Architecture
Alejandro Quintanilla, Universidad Nacional Autonoma de Mexico

Stephen Ramos, University of Maryland
Jaqueline Randall, University of North Carolina
Dru H. Schwyhart, Anderson Mason Dale Architects
Sean Solowski, Carleton University
Lauren Tindall, University of Washington
David Vilkama, Sala Architects Inc.
Gavin Yuill, Edinburgh College of Art

Ghost 9 (2007)
Architect: Ted Flato, Lake/Flato Architects; Bob Benz, Thomas Anderson & Co.
Critic: Robert McCarter, Washington University in St. Louis
Geoff Adams, University of New Mexico
David Birge, North Carolina State University
Catherine Callaway, University of Houston
Anthon Ellis, Kansas State University
Early Ewing, Portland State
Madeline Gradillas, Rick Joy Architects
Jonathan Healey, University of Maryland
Amber Howard, Texas Tech University
Jason Kerensky, Washington University in St. Louis
James Ketover, Scottsdale, AZ
Bryant Kirkland Jr., University of North Carolina at Charlotte
KC Kurtz, North Carolina State University
Sam Laffin, Dalhousie University
Erin Landsburg, University of North Carolina at Charlotte
William Layzell, University of Edinburgh
Malcolm Lee, University of Cincinnati
Mark McCormick, Edinburgh College of Art

Albert Mitchell, Washington University in St. Louis
Kristen Nakamura, University of Toronto (sponsored by Kuwabara Payne McKenna Blumberg Architects)
Brody Neville, Syracuse University
Justin Novak, Arizona State University
Daniel Perschbacher, Mississippi State University in Jackson
Marshall Prado, North Carolina State University
Spencer Purdy, University of Southern California
Ron Rochon, The Miller|Hull Partnership
Tommy Schaperkotter, University of Virginia
Aaron Senne, Washington University in St. Louis
Doron Serban, Syracuse University
Marcy Townsend, Sala Architects Inc.
Ben Trantham, University of Arkansas

For further information on participating in the Ghost Lab, please contact:

Ghost Administrator
MacKay-Lyons Sweetapple Architects Limited
2188 Gottingen Street
Halifax, NS B3K 3B4
Tel: 902-429-1867
Email: info@mlsarchitects.ca
Website: www.mlsarchitects.ca

Image Credits

All images © Brian MacKay-Lyons unless otherwise noted.

Matt Beatty 19, 22t
Adam Collins 194, 202br
Nicole Delmage 12–13, 28t, 32–33
Steven Evans 103tr, 103br, 106tr, 106br, 108–9
Selina Falvey 34
Mike Farrar 67t, 69t
Ghost 1 participant 22bl, 22br, 23, 26, 31
Ghost 3 participants 60–61, 67bl, 68br
Ghost 4 participants 84, 85bl, 89br
Ghost 5 participants 104bl, 104br
Ghost 6 participants 122br
Ghost 7 participants 144, 148, 149bl
Ghost 8 participants 166bl, 166br, 169tl, 169tr, 169bl
Karl Habermann 68t
Ken Kam 78–79, 85br, 89tl, 89bl, 90–91
Will Layzell 176t, 202t
Malcolm Lee 202bl
Etienne Lemay 98–99, 105
Kristen Nakamura 199
Courtesy of the Oxner family 67br, 110, 156, 182
Chris Oxner 40–41, 45, 48, 50–53
Chris Reardon 149tr, 149br, 150
Marriette Roodenberg 106bl
Manuel Schnell 3, 134, 176b, 179tl, 179bl, 180
Courtesy of Service Nova Scotia and Municipal Relations (SNSMR) and Natural Resources Canada 212
James Steeves 116–17, 128–29, 131–33, 140–41, 153, 155, 162–63, 166t, 169br, 172

Acknowledgments

Ghost relies on the support and collaboration of my partner, Talbot Sweetapple. It is a partnership between our practice and a loose consortium of architectural schools and practices.

Each summer the Ghost event is enriched by the contributions of a community of respected colleagues. The guest critics you have already met through their essays. The guest architects—Rick Joy, Bob Benz, Wendell Burnette, Marlon Blackwell, David Miller, and Ted Flato—were instrumental to the design and construction of the projects. The knowledge and tireless enthusiasm for the process of making architecture of the Master Builder, Gordon MacLean—the real teacher at Ghost—is humbling. Engineer Michel Comeau brings a structural rigor to each Ghost. Administrators have handled logistics with a sense of style. Then there are the "Ghosties"—the practicing architects, students, professors who *are* the Ghost Lab—participating in each Ghost project according to their skill, knowledge, and experience levels.

This book has been produced with the assistance of Beth Sanford and Adam Collins from MacKay-Lyons Sweetapple Architects. In addition, many photographers, including James Steeves, Manuel Schnell, Chris Reardon, Steven Evans, have contributed to the visual quality of this book. Many thanks to our clients and neighbors who generously put up with the disruption Ghost causes.

Finally, my family has tolerated the annual home invasions and this crazy architect's utopian vision. My wife, Marilyn, and our children, Renée, Alison, and Matthew, have been the patrons of the Ghost Lab from the beginning through a healthy combination of doubt and unconditional support.